# How Shall I Compare Thee?

## Anna E Broughton

First published in 2024 by:
Anna E Broughton

© Copyright 2024
Anna E Broughton

**ISBN: 978-1-3999-9427-9**



Printed and bound in Great Britain by:
Book Printing UK Remus House,
Coltsfoot Drive, Woodston,
Peterborough PE2 9BF

This book is dedicated to the memory of my beautiful
Mam.


*"Those who touch our lives stay in our hearts forever"*

I would like to thank my lovely family for their belief in me.

In addition I want to thank Sophie for her continuous support and patience and for keeping my spirits up and my motivation high especially during the editing process.

# Contents

# One

*T*he summer of 1947 marked a significant moment for the Broughton family as they welcomed me, Anna Elizabeth into their lives.  I was born in the front room of our Leicester home, bringing both joy and challenge to my family.  Within 24 hours of my birth, joy quickly turned to concern when Mam discovered I was haemorrhaging in my cot.  The urgency of the situation led to prompt hospitalisation.  After seven anxious days, I was returned home, safely cradled in Mam's grateful arms.  It must have been a tremendous relief for her to have her precious daughter back home after such a challenging ordeal.  It wasn't until the 1950s that newborn babies were routinely given an injection of Vitamin K to avoid such haemorrhaging.

The Broughton household consisted of my grandparents, Martha and Albert (Nana and Grandad), and their daughter, my mother, Ellen (Mam) born in 1924.  Mam had two siblings, my uncles, Ben born in 1926 and Edward in 1930.  At the time of my birth, Uncle Ben was serving in the Merchant Navy while Uncle Edward, who had bronchiectasis, a serious lung condition, continued to board at an open-air school in Western Park in Leicester.

Our home on Crafton Street, close to the heart of Leicester and just off Wharf Street, was the setting for my early years.

Wharf Street, a busy thoroughfare connecting Humberstone Gate to Russell Square, was the lifeline of many surrounding streets. It ran parallel to Clyde Street and, connecting the two, were several notable streets. Each was well known for their own speciality, including Crafton Street where you would find the Bakers Arms. Here, the latest bands would practice in the evenings in their search for stardom. Another, Erskine Street, was where we would go to buy real ice cream made on site by the Italian Cox family while Gladstone Street was known for its off licence that cornered with Clyde Street and was open until 10pm at night.

Standing proud on the corner of Wharf Street and Humberstone Gate was the Three Cranes public house which stood as a lasting symbol of the neighbourhood. This iconic establishment was more than just a pub; it was a popular haunt for both locals and visitors alike. As you entered through the pub doors you could hear the sounds of exciting boxing matches drawing a crowd of betting enthusiasts whose emotions rode high on the outcomes.

But it wasn't just boxing that stirred excitement within the pub's walls. Occasionally, the world of illegal dog fighting would rear its ugly head in the back rooms, drawing in the arm of the law.  Unwilling to turn a blind eye, the police would swoop into the premises and bring activities to an abrupt end.

On the corner of Erskine Street and Wharf Street, Birch's Electrical Store offered the latest innovations in the heart of the city.  Under the skilled ownership of Maurice Birch, the store provided an impressive array of electrical goods, bicycles, and prams, catering to the diverse needs of the community.

Next door, Lowe's fruit and veg shop overflowed with colourful and appealing displays of fresh produce. Always busy and usually working in the shop by himself, Mr Lowe always had time to say hello and sometimes he would toss an apple in the air and tell me to catch it.  If I did, I kept it!

A gentleman's hairdresser and barber shop offered a haven for grooming and relaxation away from the commotion of the street outside.  The traditional red-and-white striped pole attached to the wall outside spun gently, a symbol of a timeless service.

Mr Goodacre's hardware store welcomed customers with enthusiasm and a wealth of knowledge, while Mrs. Doris Goodacre's drapers' shop, two doors down, offered fine and stylish fabrics and cottons.  Shops that were also part of this row were the A1 Meat Co. butcher's shop and Hewitt's grocery store, where one of Mam's best friends, Bertha, worked.  Known to me as Auntie Bertha, she would always come with us if we went on a day trip on the bus.  Finally, we reach the corner of Wharf Street and Gladstone Street where Cleavers Chemist Shop was situated.

Cornering Gladstone Street on the opposite side of the road, was the historic Gaiety Theatre, its grandeur fading but its legacy enduring.  Once a principal theatrical venue, it had transformed into the Hippodrome Cinema, its walls echoing with whispers of the past.

Joseph Merrick, also known as the Elephant Man, had made his debut here in 1884, fascinating audiences with his shocking appearance but gentle presence as part of a freak show.  Though the Gaiety Theatre may have undergone many changes over the years, its walls still reverberated with the echoes of Joseph Merrick's unforgettable performance.  It is sad to think that Merrick passed away on 11th April 1890 aged just 27, his body destroyed by the hardships he had endured at the hands of Victorian exploitation.

Continuing the journey along Wharf Street towards Crafton Street was like strolling through a busy marketplace of life's essentials and indulgences, each establishment with its own uniqueness.

First in line was Leif's the Pawnbroker, its weathered '3 gold balls' symbol swinging gently.

Fortunes could be made or lost here with the exchange of treasured possessions.  Within its dimly lit interior, people's possessions filled the shelves, each holding a story waiting to be told.  Leif's played a significant role in the Broughton family's weekly routine, as it did for many other families.  Every Monday morning, Nana would join the queue outside to pawn Grandad's best suit in exchange for money to help sustain the family throughout the week.  This resourceful practice provided much-needed financial support.  However, the stakes were high: Nana would return to retrieve the suit on Fridays.  If, by chance, it had been sold, there would undoubtedly be consequences to face, adding a sense of tension to their reliance on the pawnbroker's assistance.

Just a stone's throw away, the tempting aroma of freshly baked goods wafted from Cox's Bakery, drawing passers-by like bees to nectar; the promise of warm bread and pastries filling the air.  This shop was to feature significantly in my early teenage years, shaping my experiences and memories.

Next to the alleyway leading to the bakery stood Frank Jarman's grocery store, a dependable cornerstone of the community.  Its shelves were stocked with essential provisions, providing goods to households far and wide.  From fresh produce to pantry staples, Jarman's was the heartbeat of Wharf Street, ensuring no-one went without the necessities of life.  I always called him 'Uncle Frank' maybe because I was never out of his shop, usually getting cigarettes for someone.

In the 50s most people in the area smoked, our household being no different from anyone else's.  I would be sent to buy grandad's daily supply of five Park Drive cigarettes (known as Parkies).  Even in those days it was against the law to sell cigarettes to under aged children.  However, a daily note written by grandad was all it took for Uncle Frank to exchange the money I held out for the packet of Parkies.

On the corners of Crafton Street, the cobblers' shop stood as an example of craftsmanship and tradition. Here, skilled workers laboured over worn-out shoes, breathing new life into them with each careful stitch and polish.

And finally, overlooking it all, was The Prince of Wales public house, its inviting façade beckoning weary travellers and locals alike to step inside and find respite from the busy city life.  Within its cosy interior, laughter mixed with the clink of glasses, creating an atmosphere of friendship and warmth.

With the famous clock tower in Belgrave Gate just a five-minute walk away, the neighbourhood was steeped in history, a place full of character for my upbringing.

# Two

*A*long the widely known Wharf Street, towards the busy Russell Square, there stood a quaint little shop at number 25½.  This tiny establishment belonged to none other than my great-grandmother, Lizzie, a spirited woman who had married into the Broughton family.  She and her husband, James Broughton, were the proud parents of my grandad.

The shop held a unique attraction for the menfolk of the area, as it was renowned for its supply of snuff.  Snuff, a form of smokeless tobacco, was meticulously crafted from finely ground tobacco leaves.  Men would flock to the shop to indulge in the peculiar habit of snorting or sniffing the powdered tobacco into their noses.  It delivered a potent hit of nicotine along with a tantalisingly flavoured scent.  However, there was a drawback: the unmistakably strong smell of tobacco that clung to those who indulged, often leaving their beards and moustaches stained.

It wasn't just the men who frequented Grandma Lizzie's shop.  Children, with their pockets jingling with pennies would also gather there.  With their faces pressed against the glass windows, they eagerly awaited their turn to enter and purchase a penny's worth of sweets.  Grandma Lizzie would oblige, carefully scooping out an assortment of sweets into small cone-shaped paper bags, just large enough to hold a generous two ounces of sugary delights. Such treats were very limited, of course, during the years of rationing. Once rationing was lifted, availability meant that an impressive 4oz could be bought at once, in a square bag rather than a cone.

And so, day after day, the shop at 25½ Russell Square was alive with activity. From the odour of snuff wafting through the air to the laughter of children clutching their sweet-filled bags, it was a place where the ordinary moments of life unfolded. In the simplicity of my early years, my visits to my great grandparents' shop held a special place. As a toddler, I perched upon the counter, a figure of innocence in the busyness of the shop. With a heart full of curiosity and a voice full of chatter, I greeted each customer with wide-eyed wonderment.

But as time passed, my perception changed. The once fascinating encounters with customers lost their shine, replaced by a discomfort born of grime and smell. Amid the unpleasant aroma of the shop, one element remained a constant source of fascination: the tiny scales perched upon the counter, their delicate balance was a key instrument for the precision of the trade.

While sweets beckoned from their colourful displays, my indulgence was always weakened by the

watchful eye of Grandma Lizzie.  Limited to a mere two
ounces at a time, I tasted each mouthful with restrained
pleasure.

The dimly lit living room adjoining my great-
grandparents' shop gave me shivers down my spine.  In
the corner of the gloomy back room, a painting portrayed
an angel with outstretched arms, overlooking a ladder
upon which figures ascended towards the heavens.
Grandma Lizzie explained it as a representation of a
passage to heaven, a sign of hope and redemption.  At
only 4 years old, the sight of it left me feeling unsettled,
with no real understanding of what my great
grandmother had said.

Within this dark atmosphere, I found reassurance in
the love of my great grandfather, James.  He was a
doting figure who spoiled me with secretive treats, his
indulgence a welcome respite from Grandma Lizzie's
stern face.

Deep down in my memory I hold a distinct image of
a stern but loving character, one that I will never forget.
This image of Great-grandma Lizzie, a figure of
strength, loomed large in my childhood memories
despite her passing away in 1951 when I was just four.

I look back on those formative years, my memories
painted with a mixture of nostalgia and reflection.  In the
confines of my great grandparents' shop, I discovered the

implications of human interaction, the fragility of perception, and the enduring ties of family love.  And though time may have dimmed the vividness of those childhood moments, their impression upon my life remains indelible, an example of the richness of my heritage and the journey of self-discovery that began among the counters and scales of yesteryear.

During the late 19th and early 20th century Leicester, there lived a man whose name became synonymous with delicious pies and delightful charm. His name was George but, to the people of the city, he was fondly known as 'Muggy Measures' the pie man. Little did I know it at the age of four, but this larger-than-life character was part of my family, making me part of a heritage steeped in local tradition and culinary delight.

Muggy Measures' pies were legendary, known far and wide for their savoury fillings and flaky crusts.  But it wasn't just the quality of his pies that endeared him to the people of Leicester; it was his magnetic personality and genuine warmth that made him a cherished figure in the community.

I recall hearing stories of Muggy's exploits, passed down through the generations, with pride and admiration.  I would imagine him roaming the market square in Cheapside, with his wooden tray of pies, his voice booming as he called out to passers-by, inviting them to indulge in his culinary creations.

Though I never had the chance to meet him, the legacy of Muggy Measures lived on in my family's memories. As I grew older, I couldn't help but feel a sense of pride in knowing that I was descended from such a renowned and popular figure in Leicester's history. Carrying on with my own journey through life, I always held onto the knowledge that I was part of a history rich in stories, traditions, and delicious pies.

# Three

*M*am began courting William Maltby (Bill) when she was just 17.  He was a local lad who worked for the Leicester Water Board at the Wanlip Sewage Works. Within a year, they announced their engagement which appeared to be a promising start to a future together. However, Bill's trust in Mam was shaken when he heard unfounded reports of her courting an army man.  Despite Mam's sincere commitment, Bill's doubts led him to call off their engagement suddenly.  Heartbroken and confused by his totally unexpected change of heart, Mam had no understanding of the real reason behind Bill's decision at the time.  It wasn't until many years later that she learned the truth, shedding light on this painful chapter in her past.

In May 1942, aged 18 years, Mam answered the call to support the war effort by enlisting into the Women's Land Army, leaving her home behind and venturing into the fields of a farm near Market Harborough in Leicestershire.  In this important role, she contributed to the agricultural efforts aimed at sustaining the nation during wartime, playing her part in the collective effort to support the war.  She embraced the responsibilities of working the land, driving tractors, and harvesting crops alongside her fellow Land Army girls.

Despite her skill as a hedge cutter, an accident occurred, leaving her leg badly scarred. However, regardless of the challenges, Mam created strong friendships with her companions, all young, single women seeking adventure. Their shared experiences extended beyond the fields, as they eagerly attended dances at the local barracks, where they met soldiers stationed nearby, enjoying moments of respite from their demanding work.

In 1944, during the disruption of the Second World War and another visit to the barracks, Mam's path crossed with that of Matthew Dixon, a 26-year-old handsome private from Kent. Now stationed in Leicestershire, he regularly attended the dances at the nearby barracks. Their encounter, surrounded by the chaos of wartime brought a spark of connection, igniting a budding romance in the midst of uncertainty and upheaval.

Matthew shared stories of his life before the army, painting a picture of a close-knit family and his job as a milkman. His passion for music, particularly playing the trombone in the local brass band, added depth to his character. Additionally, his cherished motorbike served as his mode of transport, offering opportunities for post-war adventures with Mam as they explored the countryside together during demobilisation. These rides became special memories, strengthening their relationship beyond the dance floor.

Hearing the jubilant celebrations of V E Day on 8th May 1945, echoing through the streets of Leicester, marking the end of World War II, Matthew and Mam found themselves caught up in a whirlwind of emotions. While the victory brought relief and joy to the country, they knew that their work was far from over.  They both remained loyal to their commitment to the war effort, supporting the transition from wartime to peacetime. For Matthew, this meant assisting with the repatriation efforts, helping returning soldiers reintegrate into civilian life and providing support to those who had been affected by the destruction of war.  His hard work earned him the respect and appreciation of his colleagues and of the community at large.  Meanwhile, Mam continued her work on the home front, ensuring that the needs of the community were met as the country began to rebuild and recover.  From organising food and clothing drives to supporting families affected by the conflict, she remained a pillar of strength and compassion in troubled times.  Whilst the country began the long road to recovery, they remained firm in their belief that a brighter future lay ahead.

In October 1946, Mam faced a distressing realisation: she was pregnant.  Overwhelmed with fear and uncertainty, she had to face the daunting prospect of breaking the news to her parents and the hardship it would bring to the family home.  Her mind raced with endless questions: What would her mother say?  What if they rejected her?  What would she tell Matthew?  The possibility of him insisting on a backstreet abortion, a dangerous practice present in many neighbourhoods, loomed threateningly.  Mam clung to the hope that Matthew loved her and would stand by her side.  The gravity of the situation left her questioning her next steps, feeling lost and alone in her uncertainty.  Matthew waited for his demobilisation papers but little did he know of the secret Mam was keeping from him.  Meanwhile, struggling with the imminent disclosure of her pregnancy, Mam was unaware of the bombshell Matthew was yet to reveal.  The impending collision of their hidden truths cast a shadow over their relationship, intensifying the uncertainty and turmoil they faced as they navigated the disruptive aftermath of the war.

Mam's world shattered as Matthew disclosed the shocking truth: he had an existing family waiting for him in Kent, a wife and 4 sons totally unaware of Mam's existence.  The news tore at the basis of the love and trust she had built with him, leaving her devastated and heart broken.

Despite her profound love for Matthew, the betrayal cut deep, leaving her unable to trust him, let alone consider marrying him.  The revelation marked the end of Mam's dream of a future for herself and Matthew and their baby.  She had to find a way to deal with the painful reality of his betrayal, and the destroyed faith in men that would haunt her for years to come.

# Four

*M*am's return home marked the beginning of a new chapter in her life, one filled with both uncertainty and consequences.  Despite the heartbreak caused by Matthew's betrayal, she found peace in the regular support from her family, her workmates and her friends, especially her dear friend, Glenis.

Glenis had been a friend to Mam since her schooldays and alongside her husband, John, they would eventually become my caring and loving godparents. With encouragement, Mam faced each day with newfound strength, gradually finding joy in the prospect of welcoming her baby into the world.  Though scarred by the dishonesty of the man she once loved, Mam's journey towards motherhood became an example of her strength and the lasting ties of family and friendship sustained her through the darkest of times.

Now, aged 23 and a woman of remarkable capability, Mam found herself navigating the complexities of single motherhood.  The social attitudes of that time period added more challenges to already difficult circumstances. The stigma surrounding illegitimate children was indeed significant, often resulting in shame for the mother and child and also for family members.

Undeterred by bad luck, Mam forged ahead, her determination to provide for me never failing.

While Mam worked long hours at a hosiery factory down the street, Nana, battling chest and breathing problems along with general ill-health, was unable to care for me during the day and so I spent my early years at the local council day nursery. Meanwhile, Grandad worked tirelessly at a local sweet factory. An average of 48 hours a week for £5/10s/0d for his efforts ensured a modest yet steady income for the family. Grandad's job was to roll out by hand the blocks of mint-flavoured boiled sugar that he would eventually cut into large pieces, then roll again and cut again, repeating this process until the sweets were transformed into what we recognise today as Fox's Glacier Mints.

Grandad had a sweet custom that was as reliable as the ticking of a clock. After his long shifts, he would return home with a handful of sweets, among which were the famous mints. These sweets, produced in Leicester, held a special place in our family. Despite their regularity, I didn't always indulge in them; perhaps they were a bit too strong for my young taste buds to fully appreciate.

Little did Grandad know that with each handful he brought home, he was contributing to a legacy far greater than he could imagine. The story of Fox's Glacier Mints, with its roots firmly planted in Leicester soil and its iconic polar bear, serves as a good example of the power of branding and the lasting impact of cultural icons. Over generations, the mints have continued to be a favourite and the brand continues to remain a best-seller in today's popular culture.

I attended a day nursery in nearby Bedford Street from the age of 1 month. I had a nurturing upbringing at the nursery, where I thrived and I enjoyed playing with my little friends and an array of toys. The routine of taking naps on tiny camp beds in the morning and the afternoon ensured I did not become overtired. I loved story time and singing and always enjoyed my meals. Part of my day nursery experience was a spoonful of cod liver oil and a small beaker of concentrated orange juice given to me twice a day. I had these at home too until I started school; I recall Mam religiously making sure I had had both. I remember seeing the sideboard cupboard full of bottles, orange juice on one side, and cod liver oil on the other. I later learned that they were provided by the NHS as part of a national drive to improve the nutrition of children in post-war Britain.

As a toddler, until the age of four, I shared a bedroom with Mam and treasured the time spent with her, reading stories and talking about my day at the nursery. But there was something that troubled me; the sound of Mam's muffled sobbing, her head buried deeply in her pillow.

"Mammy, don't cry", my innocent voice pierced through the darkness.  Mam's response was always the same, a tired sigh followed by a dismissive command.

"Go back to sleep, Anna, it's nothing, just go back to sleep."  But I couldn't simply go back to sleep when I was so upset by Mam's sorrow.  I longed to understand, to soothe the pain I sensed in Mam's tears.  Yet, my questions remained unanswered, lost in the silence of the night.

I was a pretty little girl with blonde curly hair and whose big blue eyes and smile melted the hearts of everyone I met.  Now I was about to embark on the next chapter of my life.  My upbringing was undoubtedly marked by hard work and determination, with Mam and my grandparents all contributing to the family's well-being in their own ways.  Days turned into weeks, and weeks into months, as the Broughton family faced and managed life's storms together.

# Five

*O*ur neighbourhood, characterised by its endless rows of terraced houses, was built on a strong sense of community.  The tight-knit surroundings fostered friendliness and everyone knew each other's business, creating a network of support and friendly relationships. Individuals readily helped out during significant life events such as a birth or times of loss, highlighting the closeness among the residents.  Back doors were never locked, borrowing necessities like a cup of sugar or a shilling for the meter was common, emphasising the neighbourly connections.  Despite the challenges of living in what was considered a deprived area, often commonly referred to as a slum area, the sense of community was incredibly strong, with each resident having specific roles to play in helping one another, creating a resilient and supportive environment for families like ours.

My home in Crafton Street was part of a row of houses alongside factories and pubs.  The Prince of Wales pub on the corner of the street, held warm memories of the visits with my grandparents.  Grandad, with a twinkle in his eye, would treat me to a packet of crisps and a bottle of pop in the pub yard, creating special moments that would linger in my memory.

Beyond the pub lay a series of houses heading towards the "Baker's Arm's", one of which was ours. The houses were all connected by shared entryways that lead into communal yards. It was here that the tight-knit community thrived.

As well as togetherness, there were also moments of frustration. Neighbours would gather in the shared spaces, exchanging pleasantries and catching up on the latest news and gossip as they went about their daily lives. The echoes of children's laughter and playful shouts often filled the entryway, exaggerated by its enclosed space. Complaints were often made about the noise, with some neighbours voicing their concerns about the disruption it caused to their peace and quiet. The children, including myself and the four Radley boys who shared our yard, all full of energy and mischief, would sometimes be cheeky and answer back when told off by the concerned neighbours. Our antics added another layer of liveliness to the community, but also tested the patience of those seeking a moment of peace in the middle of the city chaos.

Despite these occasional battles, the closeness of the community remained strong. Neighbours would come together to address issues and find solutions, recognising that, along with the noise and chaos, their shared space was a place they cherished.

Mam added her own colourful touch to the neighbourhood. Whilst pregnant with me and craving apples, she was once the centre of attention because she pinched one from out of the hands of a passing boy, her action bringing laughter and gossip to the tight-knit community. And when rain poured down, she'd head for the shared covered entryway, attempting to hang her laundry on the lines. She would often find them already laden with other neighbours' washing, which caused her to complain bitterly in frustration.

Towards the bottom of Crafton Street, cornered with Brougham Street, stood a busy hosiery factory, H B Howe and Son. And at the heart of this thriving industry was Mam, a woman whose dedication and expertise were woven into every seam and stitch.

From the moment she stepped foot into the factory, Mam's hands became instruments of precision and skill. Draw-threading, winding, overlocking, machining, pressing and packing, she mastered each technique with finesse, becoming a well-respected work colleague on the busy production line. Her journey in the hosiery trade was a credit to her skills and hard work.

As the years passed, Mam's role evolved. She climbed the ranks, her hard work and leadership qualities earning her the position of forelady. Guiding the workforce with firm yet compassionate hands, she ensured that every garment that left the factory was of the highest quality, a reflection of her unfaltering standards.

However, change was inevitable. In the late 1970s the winds of change swept through H B Howe and Son as it was acquired by Curzonia Knitwear. The familiar hum of machinery was soon replaced by the commotion of relocation, as the factory premises shifted to Curzon Street. Despite the upheaval, Mam remained firm, her dedication to her job and to her workmates was unaffected.

And her workmates were dedicated to her. Years later, the spring of 1974 marked a significant milestone in Mam's life: her 50th birthday. It was a Saturday and she decided to spend the day with us, making it a memorable occasion, especially for my children, Paul and Gemma. Little did Mam know, but one of the most exciting moments of her birthday was still to come, a surprise arranged by her thoughtful workmates.

Mam had a particular liking for the TV show Kojak, starring the charismatic Telly Savalas. There was something about the character's rugged charm, his trademark lollipop and iconic catchphrase, 'Who loves ya, baby?' Mam was captivated by his deep voice and his portrayal of the tough but caring detective.

On the Friday afternoon before her birthday, Mam's colleagues at the factory had secretly planned to make her day extra special.  They rallied together and joined the Telly Savalas Fan Club.  Their mission?  To obtain a large, glossy, signed photograph of Kojak himself.  Remarkably, they succeeded, not just once, but twice.

When Mam bid farewell to her workmates for the weekend, they presented her with what became her prized possessions: two highly desirable signed photographs of Telly Savalas as Kojak.  Overwhelmed with gratitude, Mam couldn't contain her excitement.

She placed one photograph proudly on her factory workbench where she could steal glances at her favourite TV detective throughout her working day.  The second photograph was carefully framed and found its place on her bedside table, a constant reminder of the thoughtful gesture from her friends.  Those glossy photographs became more than just memorabilia; they were symbols of friendship and appreciation, cherished by Mam for the rest of her days.

And so it was at the premises of Curzonia Knitwear of Curzon Street that Mam laboured daily until she finally bid farewell to a lifetime of hard work and dedication. With pride in her heart and memories to last a lifetime, she hung up her apron and retired aged 58 years, leaving behind a legacy woven into the fabric of Leicester's hosiery industry.

# Six

*I*n the middle of our row of houses stood a large
building, its imposing presence casting a shadow over
the backyards of the homes.  This building, with its main
entrance facing Wharf Street, was none other than Raven
and Co. another hosiery factory, and one that was much
bigger than Mam's further down the street.  From the
back, it dominated the neighbourhood, its windows
reflecting the sunlight in shimmering patterns.  The noise
of machinery and the occasional shouts of workers
echoed from within, a constant reminder of the activity
that boosted the local economy.

Obviously an industrial building, the factory meant
different things to the different residents of the nearby
houses.  Some found comfort in the steady hum of
productivity, a reassuring stability to their daily lives.
Others, however, had mixed feelings about the factory,
blaming the loss of open space and the intrusion of
industry on their once quiet corner of the city.
Nevertheless, Raven and Co. was an integral part of the
neighbourhood's identity.  Its history intertwined with
that of the residents, generations of families finding
employment within its walls.

It held a special attraction for me too, particularly
during the late afternoon hours when most of my friends

had gone indoors for tea.  While others settled into their evening routines, I was drawn to the street, eagerly awaiting 6pm when Mam would appear from the bottom of the street where her factory was situated.  Alone in my play, I often engaged in a game of double ball, the rhythmic bounce of the balls against the wall keeping me company until the appointed hour.

At 5pm the loud sound of the factory siren could be heard and the weary workers began to emerge towards the factory gates.  Recognising familiar faces from my street adventures, I took it upon myself to bid each worker a cheerful goodnight, a small gesture that blossomed into a nightly tradition.

It was lovely to see the workers welcoming my presence, offering kind words and occasional sweets as tokens of their appreciation.  In those short moments, I felt a sense of importance and belonging, enjoying the opportunity to connect with those who passed through the factory's back gates.  Protective of my new-found territory, I stood guard, ensuring that no-one invaded my space.

In the back streets of Leicester, as the crisp October air hinted at the arrival of autumn, I was looking for adventure.  Despite the attractiveness of Halloween and the festivities that beckoned from every corner, I knew that Mam had reservations about me taking part in such nightly exploits.  She had told me more than once, that we did not want charity and we were not beggars!  With a sigh, I accepted Mam's concerns, understanding that safety came first in her eyes.  Though I longed to roam the streets to join in the fun, I knew that Mam's worries were not unfounded, especially with the darkness of evening descending while she was still at work.

Although disappointed at missing out on Halloween, I was more excited about Bonfire Night, just around the corner on 5th November.  As preparations began in earnest, my friends and I seized upon the opportunity to participate in the time-honoured tradition of building a bonfire.  With plenty of derelict sites scattered nearby, finding materials for our bonfire was no challenge at all.  An old pram, discarded amongst the rubble and debris of Wharf Street, became our makeshift buggy, filled to the brim with salvaged planks of wood.  The bonfire grew bigger and better and so too did our enthusiasm, intensified by the prospect of a blazing spectacle to light up the night sky.  But the bonfire was only part of the festivities; another tradition awaited our attention, the creation of a Guy Fawkes.

Sharing our resources, we embarked on a creative venture, fashioning a puppet from discarded materials. With nimble fingers and boundless imagination, we shaped the figure using old newspapers, rags, and worn-out clothing.  Together, we carefully assembled the limbs and crafted a head, striving for an uncanny resemblance.

My ever-supportive Mam contributed to our project, giving us a Guy Fawkes mask to lend authenticity to our creation.  We added a sign, 'Penny for the Guy', then ventured into the streets, so excited and proud of our efforts.

One evening, while I waited for my friends to finish their tea, I decided to take up my usual position at the factory gates with Guy Fawkes at my side.  I watched the factory workers emerge from their daily toil, their weary faces illuminated by the soft glow of streetlamps.  The air crackled with the energy of Bonfire Night, increasing the excitement.  To my astonishment, as the workers passed by, they generously threw coins into my grandfather's cap, placed in the makeshift pram alongside the Guy.  The sound of metal against fabric filled the air, a symphony of spontaneous giving.  For a brief but magical moment, I stood captivated by the outpouring of generosity.  It dawned on me that the workers, flushed with their weekly wages, were happy to share their hard-earned cash with me.  Each coin symbolised their appreciation for my makeshift spectacle.

The evening wore on.  As the workers dispersed, I was amazed at the scene before me.  The cap overflowed with coins.  Here, glimmering in the streetlamp's faint light, was a shining example of the kindness and goodwill of those who had contributed.  With a wide grin on my face, I gathered up the coins, surprised by and grateful for the unexpected windfall.  It was a moment I would never forget, reminding me yearly of the power of people's generosity and the magic of Bonfire Night.  I made my way home, my pockets jingling with my new-found wealth, and I knew that this year's celebrations would be truly unforgettable.

I couldn't wait for Mam to return home from work. Clutching tightly to the bag of coins I had collected earlier that evening, I could barely contain myself.  It was a special gift, one I had decided to keep secret until the perfect moment.  With help from Nana, I counted the money and it came to a total of £1/10s/6d.  What an amazing amount!

Mam entered the living room, tired after a long day's work but happy it was the weekend.  I couldn't contain my excitement any longer.  With a wide grin, I pushed the bag of coins into Mams hands, the weight of their contents evidence of the generosity of the factory workers.

Mam's eyes widened in astonishment as she peered into the bag, disbelief flickering across her face.

"What on earth is this? Where did you get all of this money from?" she asked.

With a proud smile, I explained how I had collected the money from the workers at the factory, explaining how I had been encouraged by the tradition of Penny for the Guy. I was full of pride as I told her about my solo effort, my determination evident in every word.

Listening intently, Mam's heart swelled with pride at my initiative and resourcefulness. Yet, beneath her admiration, a pang of uncertainty lingered. The coins represented a significant sum, one that could make a difference in our lives, but all I wanted was for Mam to take the money to enjoy for herself. After a moment's hesitation, Mam made a decision. With a huge smile, she told me that I was indeed a lucky girl and encouraged me to keep the money, assuring me that I deserved it for my hard work and resourcefulness. However, as I continued to insist, Mam finally agreed to keep the money in safe keeping.

My face lit up with joy as I realised that my gift had been accepted. With a sense of newfound independence, I began to dream of all the possibilities that lay ahead, knowing that I had the power to make a difference in my own life.

We sat together in the warmth of our home, the bag of coins serving as a reminder of my determination to help in any way I could, and of the relationship between mother and daughter. Mam couldn't help but marvel at the remarkable young woman I was becoming.

The next day, when my friends and I trundled along the streets for the last time, our pram laden with wood and our Guy Fawkes proudly on display, I felt a rush of satisfaction that made me shout out,

"Penny for the Guy, please!" even louder than ever before.  Though I may have missed out on Halloween, the promise of Bonfire Night and the togetherness of my friends filled me with a sense of adventure that no amount of Halloween sweets could match.  Having reached our destination, ready to light the bonfire and begin the festivities, I was unaware that the memories we were creating would last a lifetime.

# Seven

*T*he fronts of the identical houses reflected the similarity of their interiors.  Each dwelling boasted two cosy reception rooms, a well-equipped kitchen, and an outdoor toilet.  Ascending the narrow staircase led to a trio of snug bedrooms, where dreams took flight from the humdrum of everyday life.

At number 6 was Violet, a nice lady who was younger than most of the neighbours.  She lived alone in a very 'posh' house and she also sounded posh to me, but I liked her very much.  If she invited me in for whatever reason I would notice how clean and light her house was, particularly the hallway, or 'the passage', as we called it.  On a table in her passage, she had a set of three mini books, held together on a little silver rack, one of which was a dictionary.  They were in immaculate condition and I absolutely loved them.  She also had a telephone, unlike the rest of us in the street.  She told the nearby neighbours they could use it but no-one ever did; if we needed a phone, we would use the one at the pub or the phone box next to the newly built telephone exchange on Wharf Street.  I can't remember Violet's surname as she always insisted I called her Violet.  Whether she was truly posh or not, in my eyes she was a model of elegance with her polished speech, office job and a beautifully maintained home. She even had a carpet in the front room!

Mrs Howkins lived at number 10. She never sat outside her back door, but, if I was passing through her yard and she was in her kitchen, she would wave and occasionally invite me in to give me a treat, either a few sweets or a freshly baked rock cake.

On the other hand, next door to Mrs Howkins was Mrs Anderson. Her Christian name was Ada but I would never have dared call her that; she was only ever Mrs Anderson. I always knew when Mrs Anderson was sitting outside her back door because I could hear the sound of her knitting needles clicking together. This had its benefits because it warned me to go quietly as I passed through the entry; if anyone was going to tell me off for making a racket, it would be her. Mrs Anderson seemed a bit of an ogre to me but Mam always said what a lovely lady she was. Her days were filled with the gentle rhythm of household chores and the laughter of her children. Beneath the quiet of her home lay a place of refuge forged by wartime necessity. For, like everyone else in the street, Mrs Anderson had a cellar.

Our cellar was accessed through a door in the living room, and down a flight of stairs. There was a chute from a grate in the pavement, next to the front doorstep, into a compartment where the coal man emptied his sacks of coal. Split into two areas, the cellar served not only as a storage space but also as a shelter from the perils of war.

During my childhood, the events of the war were still very fresh in people's minds, often a topic of conversation. Just like any other mother of the time, Mam would insist that I should be seen and not heard so, by sitting just out of sight and as quiet as a mouse, I would often manage to eavesdrop on these stories as the neighbours remembered key events. I learned that, as the conflict raged outside, Mrs. Anderson and her neighbours, including our family, would find relief and safety in their cellars. Small holes knocked into the cellar walls served as passages of escape, bridging the divide between neighbouring families. This simple measure ensured that if anyone found their exit blocked by bomb damage, they would always be able to get out through another house. When darkness fell and the air raid sirens sounded, the community would rush into their underground hiding places.

The night of November 19, 1940, came to be known as the Leicester Blitz. The city was draped in darkness, its streets silent and watchful. War had cast its shadow over the city, but no-one could foresee the horrors that would develop that night. As the clock struck midnight, calm became chaos. The German planes descended upon Leicester, the noise deafening, the devastation horrendous.

Surrounded by thunderous explosions and the wail of sirens, the people of Leicester scrambled for cover. In those agonising moments, our eight houses on our single street displayed united toughness.  Mrs Anderson, our family, and our neighbours sought refuge together in the cellars, in the safety of their underground shelter.

When dawn finally broke, it revealed a city reduced to rubble, streets impassable, and lives shattered.  The number of people who perished that night was devastating, with one hundred and eight people losing their lives.  Through the ruins, the residents emerged, their hearts strengthened by the knowledge that they were never alone in their suffering.  In time, the people of Leicester came together, to rebuild their shattered city, brick by brick.

During my childhood in the 1950s, the world was still struggling through the aftermath of the war.  Money was tight for the country; money was tight for families. My peers and I lived in a time very different from the one enjoyed by children today.  The simplest of pleasures were difficult.  Sugar was a scarce commodity due to rationing until 1953 while meat only became freely available a year later.  Families had to make do with less, stretching their wages to make ends meet. With the need for another wage being more essential than the classroom, many youngsters found themselves launched into the workforce at just 14 years of age.

Opportunities for further education were limited to the privileged few.

Abandoned houses and war-damaged sites weren't just neglected spaces, they were openings to adventure and imagination. With boundless energy and curiosity, these landscapes became playgrounds. Though remnants of destruction, these sites held endless possibilities for me and my friends. Here, amid the rubble, broken furniture and twisted bed springs we would build dens, make up stories of daring escapades, and embark on grand adventures.

My leisure activities were a far cry from the digital distractions of today. Radio broadcasts filled the airwaves, offering entertainment and news updates to eager listeners. Board games and card games provided hours of amusement, encouraging family and friendly rivalries.

In place of fast-food joints and streaming services, pleasures were simpler. A trip to the local fish and chip shop was a rare treat, enjoyed by families on special occasions. The family home served as a shelter from the outside world, albeit one filled with backbreaking household chores and daily struggles.

Wash day in the early 1950s was a formidable task, a weekly chore that demanded patience, perseverance, and no shortage of elbow grease. While most households opted for Monday as their designated wash day, our kitchen was witness to a different routine; a Friday evening ritual that spilled over into Saturday, organised by none other than Mam herself.

A brick-built copper stood in the corner of our modest kitchen, a relic of times past and one that Mam never dared to use. Instead, she relied on a more basic method to tackle the week's accumulation of dirt and grime.

As the evening approached, Mam would ignite the gas stove, setting a procession of water-filled white tin buckets to boil. Her experienced hands poured the scalding water into the shallow, elongated sink that had seen its fair share of uses, from washing to bathing me as a child.

With the water steaming and ready, Mam plunged into the task at hand. She worked tirelessly, washing soap into the fibres, soaking and scrubbing the garments, kneading out the stains and wear of daily life. Once saturated, the laundry would rest overnight, soaking in the cleansing waters, ready for the next phase come morning.

As dawn broke on Saturday, Mam wasted no time in resuming her chores. With the washing now ready for its final clean, she meticulously scrubbed each article of clothing on a wooden washboard, coaxing out the remnants of soap and scum.  A cold-water rinse followed, a sharp contrast to the warmth that had preceded it, before the laundry was taken into the yard for its rendezvous with the mangle.

The mangle was a distinguished piece of equipment that we shared with our neighbour Dottie.  It loomed large in the corner of the yard, its metal rollers standing as guardians of cleanliness.  With neat movements, Mam fed the damp clothes through the mangle's rollers and turned the crank, each rotation squeezing out excess moisture until the fabric ran smooth and nearly dry.

With a last final push, the clean laundry was pegged to the line, a colourful array of garments fluttering in the breeze, a credit to Mam's hard work and the timeless ritual of wash day in the 1950s.

With refrigerators still considered a luxury, daily shopping trips were a necessity rather than a convenience.  Housewives worked hard, handwashing clothes and managing the household, while their husbands ventured out into the world of paid employment.  For my family and countless others, the 1950s were a time of enforced hardiness, resourcefulness, and a firm determination to find a positive outlook alongside the hardships.

One evening during dinner, Mam realised she had run out of vinegar to accompany the delicious piece of fish she was preparing.  She asked me to go to Dottie's to borrow a cup of vinegar, promising to replace it by the weekend.

"OK, I'll be back in a minute," I replied, heading out on my errand.  However, I took longer than expected to return, causing Mam to wonder what had happened to me.  When I finally arrived home, I had a bottle of vinegar in my hand instead of a cup.  Curious, Mam asked how I had ended up with a bottle and why it had taken me so long.  I explained that the shop was crowded, and I had to wait my turn in the queue.  Mam then realised that I had misunderstood her and gone to Dottie Smith's chip shop at the top of Wharf Street, instead of going to Dottie's house next door!  Feeling embarrassed by my actions, Mam apologised to the chip shop owner the next day, ensuring that the misunderstanding was cleared up and the vinegar was paid for.  The incident became a source of laughter in the household, with Mam often retelling the story to friends and family, much to my humiliation.  It became a comical story that we would repeat many times in the years to come.

During post-war rationing, every bit of food became a precious commodity for Mam and our family.  With supplies scarce and strict limits on what could be purchased, Mam had to be inventive, stretching the rations to feed us.

Lavish birthday parties and extravagant celebrations were unheard of.  Instead, Mam had to find ways to mark special occasions with the limited resources she had.  The shelves of the local grocers were often bare, with basics like sugar, butter, and flour in short supply.  Planning for a birthday party or a special occasion, Mam faced the harsh reality that many traditional treats were simply out of reach both financially and because of the family ration allowances.  A cake decorated with layers of icing and a display of candles seemed like a distant dream, replaced instead by simpler, more modest offerings.

Mam refused to let post-war rationing dampen the spirits of her family.  With creativity and resourcefulness, she found many ways to make the most of what she had.  Perhaps it was a home-made fruit crumble in place of a sweet dessert or a savoury pie filled with seasonal vegetables instead of meat.

For Mam and her family, post-war rationing may have made hosting a birthday party or special occasion difficult, but it also served as a reminder of the importance of the simple things in life, even in the most challenging of times.

# Eight

*D*uring my preschool years, the time spent with my Nana grew with each passing day.  Nana's illness progressed slowly, making it difficult for her to breathe at times.  A bed was set up in the front room of our cosy house, allowing her to remain as independent as possible and rest more comfortably.  I was so delighted because this meant that my dear Nana was now downstairs, within easy reach for cuddles and chats whenever I pleased.  Every morning before nursery and upon returning home, I made a beeline for the front room, eager to spend quality time with Nana.

Our home was full of the domestic aromas of cooking and cleanliness, but one odour lingered and I disliked it immensely.  It was the prevailing smell of kaolin poultice simmering away on the gas stove.  Nana's health demanded it, requiring the poultices to be applied to her chest at least twice a day but, no matter whether one was actively boiling on the cooker or not, the unmistakable smell of kaolin seemed to occupy every corner of the house.  As the poultice bubbled and steamed on the stove, its chalky, earthy scent filled the air, mingling with the everyday smells of home and family, a constant presence that was impossible to ignore.  For Nana, the poultice was a lifeline, a soothing ointment for her chest, providing relief from the discomfort of her condition. It reminded me of Nana's struggle with illness, a struggle that I found difficult to understand.

The front room was also home to an upright piano, once played by Nana with skill and precision. It now stood silent, out of bounds to avoid disturbing her rest. The temptation to tinker with the keys was always with me but I understood the importance of keeping the room quiet and peaceful for Nana.

By the time I reached preschool age, my Uncle Ben had already embarked on a new chapter of his life. No longer at sea, he was now happily married to June with two children of their own, Colin and Jennifer. Colin, just ten months younger than me, shared my blonde-coloured curly hair. Although he didn't visit the house very often, we would quickly become engrossed in play when he did.

Colin and I were both still under the age of five and we were strictly confined to the safety of the front doorstep. However, our imaginations knew no bounds despite this limitation. It wasn't long before the neighbouring children caught wind of the fun happening on Nana's doorstep and eagerly joined in, laughter filling the air and the sound of little feet jumping about. We all joined together to enjoy the adventures created by our young imaginations, making memories to last a lifetime.

On 6th February 1952, the sudden and unexpected death of King George VI sent shock waves through the residents of Crafton Street, casting a sad mood over the neighbourhood and the world at large.  As the news spread, neighbours gathered at Mrs. Anderson's house seeking composure and understanding in each other's company.  The radio served as a lifeline, broadcasting the unfolding events of the day.  Over cups of tea, neighbours listened intently, their minds swirling with questions about the sudden and tragic loss and its implications for the future.  Nevertheless, there were few answers to be found in those early moments.  As the nation plunged into mourning, the period of uncertainty gave way to the proclamation of King George VI's eldest daughter, Queen Elizabeth II, as the new monarch. Filled with profound sadness, the people of Crafton Street, like the rest of the world, prepared themselves for the dawn of a new era under the reign of their young queen.

The summer of 1952 approached and my fifth birthday loomed on the horizon, marking the beginning of a new chapter in my young life.  With the disruption of starting infant school just a few weeks away, I was both excited and nervous.  The prospect of a new school still filled me with apprehension despite having attended day nursery for all of my early years.  My morning cuddles with Nana provided me with an opportunity to express my reluctance to leave the familiarity of home and nursery and head for the unknown territory of school.

Before my school adventure could begin, I had something to look forward to: a holiday visit to my endearing godparents, Auntie Glenis and Uncle John. I adored these visits because they meant escaping to the countryside, where trees, birds, and a sprawling garden awaited my eager exploration.

As a child growing up in a busy city, Birstall always seemed like a far-off land to me. The journey feeling like an adventure into the unknown despite it being a mere four miles away. Uncle John, behind the wheel of his trusty green Ford Prefect, made me feel like royalty as we set off on our journey leaving behind the noisy streets and towering buildings. The air seemed fresher, the sky bluer, and the world felt more alive, and full of bird song. Tall trees lined the winding lanes, their branches swaying gently in the breeze and fields stretching out as far as the eye could see.

My fascination with Uncle John's beehives knew no bounds. Every visit to the top of the garden to see the hives triggered my curiosity about the busy world of bees and the wonders of nature. During one of my visits on a scorching hot day, while I was absorbed in play on the lawn, I suddenly felt a sharp piercing feeling on my arm. With a cry of pain, I realised I had unknowingly disturbed a bee, laying my arm directly in its path. My cries filled the air, echoing across the road, but Uncle John swiftly came to my aid. With calm reassurance, he applied a soothing ointment to the sting, gently easing my discomfort. As the ointment took effect, the pain began to subside, and my fear changed into gratitude for my uncle's quick response. Though the sting served as a painful reminder of the need for caution around the beehives, it did little to dampen my enthusiasm for the fascinating world of bees.

Uncle John was a window cleaner and was a well-known sight in the Birstall neighbourhood, his tall frame perched precariously on his bicycle as he rode off into the early morning light. Balancing a set of long, heavy ladders on the side of his bike, he seemed to defy gravity with each push on the pedals. I often found myself marvelling at his ability, wondering how he managed to ride his bike through the streets with such an awkward load.

Auntie Glenis was not only a talented seamstress but also a generous person who held a special place in my heart. Whenever Mam found herself needing a new dress for me, Auntie Glenis would come to the rescue, transforming discarded garments into beautiful outfits that were both stylish and practical. Mam was very grateful for Auntie Glenis's kindness, knowing that her handmade dresses not only saved money, easing the burden of providing for her family, but also allowed me to feel special and well-dressed.

Every time Auntie Glenis made me a new dress, it was like receiving a gift from a fairy godmother. I would twirl and spin in excitement, my eyes sparkling with joy. Wearing the clothes Auntie Glenis had made for me was proof that the power of friendship transformed even the simplest of things into something truly magical.

On one unforgettable visit, Auntie Glenis invited me to be her model for the day. This was so exciting! Barbara and Norman, another of Mam's dear friends, were soon to become Mr and Mrs Green, and they had chosen me to be one of their bridesmaids, the second time I had had this honour. Auntie Glenis was also a close friend of Barbara's so she had been asked to make the bridesmaids outfits, including my own. I slipped into the exquisite bridesmaid dress and I felt like a princess, imagining the upcoming winter wedding. The prospect filled me with excitement, especially after this fitting where I had fallen in love with my outfit. My dress, a stunning creation of long red velvet with delicate short sleeves, made me feel like the prettiest girl in the world. Paired with white fluffy earmuffs, a matching shawl and a white muff to keep my hands warm, I couldn't wait to walk down the aisle in style on the magical day ahead.

Life with Auntie Glenis and Uncle John was very different from my experiences at home, though I felt happy in both settings.  The sprawling garden became my playground, where I'd roam among the flowers, picking daisies from the lawn to weave into a daisy chain for Auntie Glenis.  Teatime was a special treat.  We would have egg and cress sandwiches, cut into perfectly triangular shapes, followed by a tin of fruit cocktail topped with evaporated milk all served on delicate china that made me feel like a grown-up.

My bedroom in Birstall was warm, cheerful and very comfortable.  The walls were covered with pretty floral wallpaper, and Uncle John had put up shelves for my favourite dolls and books.  Unlike at home, I had the luxury of taking a proper bath whenever I pleased.  Back home, baths were reserved for Sundays, with the old tin bath placed in front of a crackling fire.  On other days of the week, I had to have a good strip wash standing in the kitchen sink, something I detested.

Despite the fun I had during my time with Auntie Glenis and Uncle John, I couldn't help but miss my Mam and Nana.  I always looked forward to Friday evenings when Uncle John would take me to pick up Mam.  The occasions were filled with laughter and warmth as Mam joined us in the countryside retreat.  Together, we embarked on adventures, exploring the beautiful views of the countryside and basking in the calmness of nature.

One of our favourite activities was having a picnic by the river, where we would enjoy home-made treats and share stories of our week apart.  As I grew older, my holidays with Auntie Glenis and Uncle John were some of the most special times I had experienced during my childhood.

# Nine

*T*he much-anticipated day had finally arrived: I started infant school. With new clothes and shoes lovingly chosen by Mam, I felt a flicker of excitement mixed with a tense expectation. Mam, taking the morning off work, proudly escorted me, radiating love and affection.

As we approached the doors of Taylor Street Infant and Junior School, my emotions were getting the better of me. Sensing my apprehension, Mam wrapped me in a reassuring hug, her words filled with encouragement and enthusiasm. With a final goodbye I entered the school, waving my hand vigorously to my anxious Mam.

Inside the bustling school, I had entered a whole, new, un-known world. The corridors echoed with the shuffling of feet as my classmates hurriedly made their way to the toilets, all seemingly synchronised in their bodily needs. This sight left me bewildered, a striking contrast to the quiet isolation of home.

There was one ritual that stood out in the organised chaos of school life: the daily distribution of school milk. It would begin as the bell signalled playtime, and the classroom buzzed with expectation. Students eagerly lined up, their hands outstretched, reaching for the small bottles of milk that awaited them. I watched in fascination as the bottles were handed out, each one containing a valuable portion of extra nourishment. While some of my classmates wrinkled their noses at the prospect of drinking the milk, I was thrilled. There was something comforting about the routine, something reassuring in its simplicity. Holding my bottle tightly, I felt a sense of familiarity because I was used to enjoying this daily ritual at day nursery. In this strange, new environment, with a multitude of new faces and the commotion of different activities, the school milk became my mainstay, a familiar constant in an ever-changing world. My fondness for the milk set me apart from my classmates who often grumbled about its taste and texture. With each sip, I felt myself growing more accustomed to this new chapter of my life, finding a new confidence in my school experience.

In post-war Britain, where every provision counted, school milk held a special significance. It was introduced to boost children's diets. The small bottles of milk became an essential commodity in schools across the country. Even during the harsh winters, the tradition continued. Crates of milk stood outside school gates their silver tops standing on columns of frozen milk pushing above the surface.

My teacher, Mrs. Johnson, a firm believer in the benefits of milk, didn't mince her words when it came to its consumption. Addressing the more reluctant drinkers with a stern tone of voice, she would tell them off, insisting that:

"Milk is good for you, child. You WILL drink it all up!" And so, alongside the everyday routines of school life and the bitter cold of winter, I found a small pleasure in my daily drink of milk.

I grasped the routines of school life with curiosity and determination.  Sitting at small desks to do colouring and engaging in new games with my newfound friends during playtime was very enjoyable.  Despite my initial apprehension, I quickly adjusted to the rhythms of school life, grabbing the opportunity to learn and explore alongside my classmates.  With each day, my enthusiasm for school grew, bringing with them new discoveries and adventures in the fascinating world of infant education.

Excitement filled the air in my school at the prospect of the new queen's coronation.  It reached its peak with just a few days left until the grand event on Tuesday, June 2nd, 1953, when preparations were in full swing. The classrooms were decorated with red, white and blue bunting and streamers, setting the stage for a celebration fit for royalty.  I, like my classmates, was bubbling with excitement as we eagerly awaited the historic day.  On the momentous day, the school came alive with festivities, and I joined my classmates on the steps of the school entrance for a special photo shoot to commemorate the occasion.  Among the many jubilant faces, I was luckily sitting beside my best friend, Carol, who insisted on sharing this memorable moment together.

My friendship with Carol blossomed, encouraged by shared experiences and mutual interests.  Through laughter, adventures, and the ups and downs of school life, our friendship grew stronger with each passing day. We enjoyed the pleasures and challenges of childhood together, and on that historic day of the queen's coronation, including the cheers and celebrations, our friendship was sealed, certain to endure the test of time.

In the wake of the historic coronation, the residents of Crafton Street came together to celebrate in true British style with a grand coronation street party.  The entire street was covered with colourful decorations of red, white and blue, echoing the patriotic spirit that swept the nation.  Each neighbour contributed to the festivities, preparing an array of tasty treats and goodies to share.  The tables groaned under the weight of the amount of food, with dishes ranging from traditional sandwiches and savoury pies to sweet treats and cakes, all featuring the colours of the Union Flag.  Once everyone had had plenty to eat, the party atmosphere reached new heights with a series of lively games and activities.  Laughter filled the air as children and adults alike participated in sack races, egg and spoon races, and tug-of-war competitions, their competitive spirits ignited by the wonderful occasion. The street, indeed the whole country, let its hair down.

The babies and toddlers, exhausted from a day filled with laughter and excitement, were gently taken indoors to their beds. But for us older kids, the night was still young and we sat on our doorsteps, watching the adults, eager to soak in every moment of the celebrations but careful not to make ourselves conspicuous in case we, too, were sent to bed. It meant that we had to giggle very quietly at the sight of Mrs Anderson dancing with Mr Howkins, and of Mrs Howkins not being particularly happy about it!

From our vantage point, we watched as our families twirled and swayed to the rhythm, their laughter ringing out like bells in the night. The adults raised glasses of beer and stout, toasting to our new queen and wishing her a reign full of happiness and good health. Fred Wilson, landlord of the Prince of Wales pub, made sure that we kids did not miss out. He treated us to several crates of fizzy pop and boxes of Smith's crisps with their little blue bag of salt inside. Despite the differences that may have divided us on any other day, tonight we were united in our shared love for our country and our monarch.

# Ten

*M*am found herself in a recognisable predicament as my sixth birthday approached.  Like any other child I had a laundry list of birthday wishes, but the family's financial situation was far from obliging.  Determined to make my day special regardless, Mam wracked her brain for a solution.

One afternoon, while strolling past Rowbothams doll and pram shop on Belvoir Street, my eyes lit up like fireworks at the sight of a particular doll.  It was a magnificent creation, standing a proud 30 inches tall with a lifelike appearance that was truly captivating.  What caught my heart was its unique feature: when held by its two arms, the doll could take steps, a marvel of engineering that fascinated me.

Mam knew she had found the perfect gift even though it would put a strain on her budget.  The doll, with its lifelike movements and comforting presence, would be more than just a toy; it would be a much-loved companion for me.  As I unwrapped my birthday present, my excitement knew no bounds.  The doll, now christened Susan, became my closest friend, and we were inseparable.

Mam couldn't help but notice how my world seemed to expand with the addition of my new companion.  Yet she also recognised a need for me to socialise more with children of my own age.  Observing my attachment to the doll, Mam had an epiphany.  It was time for me to spread my wings beyond the confines of our home, to mingle and play with other children.  Not only would this boost my social skills, but it would also enhance my childhood in ways that no doll could replicate.  With gentle encouragement, Mam guided me towards new friendships, helping me realise that while Susan was a wonderful companion, there was a world of adventures waiting beyond the safety of our home.

My birthday party was a whirlwind of laughter, games, and the warm embrace of loved ones.  Among the guests were usual faces that I loved.  Uncle Edward and Auntie Mary were there.  Seeing them brought back memories of their wedding day the previous year when I had played an important part of being their bridesmaid.  As I caught sight of them across the room, memories flooded back, the fluttering excitement as I walked down the aisle, the gentle reassurance of Auntie Mary's hand in mine, and the proud smile on Uncle Edward's face.  Their presence brought back the magic of that day, reminding me of the love and happiness that surrounded us all.

Nevertheless, the happiness didn't end there. Uncle Ben arrived with Auntie June, Colin and Jennifer, and Auntie Glenis and Uncle John arrived holding a rather large chocolate-covered birthday cake. Along with Mam, Nana and Grandad, the day painted a picture of the love and support that surrounded me. Mam spared no effort to ensure my birthday was a celebration to remember. Realising I was growing up, Mam made an announcement. She said that I would now be allowed to play outside more often and to explore the world beyond our doorstep. Little did everyone know, this decision would lead to an unexpected surprise that would soon be revealed, one that would shape my childhood in ways they could never have imagined.

A sudden knock on the back door interrupted the festivities. Curious and surprised, Mam opened the door to find three of her work colleagues from the knitwear factory where she worked tirelessly. They were holding a shiny, brand-new blue bike, a sight that left her momentarily speechless. Mam's friends explained that the people at the factory wanted to contribute to making my birthday extra special. They had pooled their resources to fulfil my heartfelt wish for a bicycle. Now overcome with emotion, and moved beyond words, Mam found tears welling in her eyes at the unexpected display of kindness and generosity.

Mams voice rang out through the house, calling for me to come and see the surprise waiting for me at the back door. Curious and excited, I hurried over. I was met with a scene that took my breath away. There, gleaming in the sunlight, stood a magnificent blue bike. Overcome with emotion, I couldn't find the words to express my gratitude.  Instead, tears of joy streamed down my cheeks as I embraced each of the ladies tightly, their faces beaming with happiness at my reaction.

"Thank you, thank you, thank you!" I shouted, my excitement fizzing like pop.  My birthday, already filled with love and laughter, now felt complete with this unexpected and treasured gift.

With my new bike in tow, my mind raced with possibilities, but who would show me how to ride? Thankfully, Uncle Edward came to the rescue, offering to take me to the nearby waste ground on Lee Circle to teach me, the start of my thrilling new adventures.  With patience and commitment, especially on Uncle Edward's part, I was determined to master the skill of riding my new bicycle.  And yes, eventually Uncle Edward let go, ready for me to discover a world I hadn't yet experienced.  As I pedalled off with Uncle Edward by my side, the golden rays of the evening sky reflected the warmth in my heart.  Could this day truly get any better?

At the tender age of six, I grasped this new freedom of childhood with boundless energy and enthusiasm. Stepping out of my house, I couldn't wait to join the lively gathering of neighbourhood kids, ready to immerse myself in the thrill of play.  The streets, our endless playground, stretched out before us, full of limitless possibilities, and my front doorstep became an assembly point for all those seeking adventure.

The doorstep symbolised more than just an entrance; it was an extension of the home's hospitality, a space where the heart of the community thrived. Whilst I skipped through the streets with my friends, the attraction of the doorstep was irresistible. Pausing in my play, I often joined the gatherings, eager to be part of the lively conversations.

Doorsteps weren't merely places to sit; they were the bustling centres of neighbourhood life. With warmer days bathing the streets in sunlight, a lively sound of laughter and conversation echoed through the neighbourhood. People gathered on their doorsteps, engaged in gossip and tales of everyday life, forming a colourful picture of shared experiences. Here, women would knit away, their nimble fingers working busily as they kept watch over their children at play. The image of an elderly man, settled comfortably on his doorstep, pipe in hand, engaged in deep conversation with his neighbour, was a normal and comforting sight. Prams lined the pavements, visible proof of the abundance of young life within the community. Wide-eyed babies and curious toddlers peeked out from their cosy shelters while their mothers exchanged news and laughter with neighbours.

Such an important place needed to be kept clean. Meet the Donkey Stone!

Donkey Stones, those unassuming symbols of household pride, were treasured possessions. You got them from the 'Rag-n-Bone' man in exchange for unwanted items. These old-fashioned scouring stones, decorated with a distinctive donkey imprint, were crafted from a cement-like mixture into a soft stone. Their tones, ranging from light brown to yellow, pale cream, or white, held significance beyond simple practicality. The colour chosen by the housewife was believed to signify the family's status in society: a deep yellow stone for a factory worker, while a man of white-collar status might opt for pale cream or white.

The ritual of scouring with a Donkey Stone was a weekly affair for Mam, including not only the front and the rear steps of our home but even the windowsills and back alleyways. 'Doing the step' wasn't just a chore; it was an opportunity for friendship and community. Neighbours would chat, exchanging gossip and stories as they meticulously cleaned their doorsteps. Beneath the cover of friendly chatter lay a silent competition, with each woman striving to outshine the other in a subtle game of one-upmanship.

The tradition of Donkey Stones slowly faded into obscurity, becoming a relic of a bygone era. However, I was hardly aware of them. I was enjoying timeless pastimes handed down through generations.  Whip and top, hopscotch, double ball, and skipping became my cherished companions, taking me away to a world of endless fun and imagination.

'Double ball' was at the top of my list of favourite games.  The area of pavement in front of my house was as known to me as the lino in the living room.  I knew every crack, every dent, every smooth patch and exactly how many paces I would take to reach the curb.  With each throw and catch, I sharpened my skills until I became a street champion, mastering the delicate balance of skill and precision, with the singular goal of never dropping the balls.

In the rhythmic dance of double ball, I enjoyed both the challenge and pleasure.  With practised ease, I would launch each ball towards the wall, my movements fluid and sure.  As the balls rebounded, I caught them with accuracy, my focus remaining constant even with the sound of cheers and chants.

Double ball wasn't just about dexterity; it was a symphony of song and motion.  With each throw, my friends and I sang rhymes that guided our movements, adding an extra layer of excitement to the game.

"Matthew, Mark, Luke and John," we sang.  "Please will the next one carry on?"  And carry on we did, each verse encouraging our determination to keep the rhythm alive.  Through the ups and downs, the triumphs and near misses, my friends and I persevered, united in our quest for victory.

Years passed, but my love for Double Ball remained. Even as I entered my early teens, I continued to grace the streets with my presence, an acknowledgement of my lasting passion for the game.  In those moments of play, I found not just competition, but togetherness; not just skill, but joy.  For in the world of Double Ball, every throw and every catch were a celebration of friendship, skill, and the boundless spirit of youth.

I wasn't alone in my love for these traditional games. In a locality where the streets were almost devoid of traffic, the children of the community enjoyed the pleasure of freedom in the open spaces.  We enjoyed a variety of activities that characterised our era.

The smaller children found endless fascination in toy prams and dolls, breathing life into their make-believe worlds.  Inspired by the nurturing roles they witnessed, they embraced the joys of caregiving, just as I had done in years past.

British Bulldog filled us older children with laughter as we dashed across the pavement, dodging the determined chase of the 'bulldog'.

Hopscotch squares covered the flag stones, inviting nimble feet to hop and jump.  In the afternoons, the girls would gather on the pavement, chalk in hand, ready to create their own adventures.  With skilled strokes, they drew the hopscotch grids onto the rough surface of the ground, each square transformed dull slabs into vibrant canvases, each stroke of chalk an example of youthful creativity.

Hopping along the chalk-drawn squares, my new-found friend Susan from 46 Crafton Street, and I had immense fun.  Hopscotch wasn't merely a game; it was a door to a world where imagination reigned supreme.  We would dance across the pavement, our friendship solidified by shared laughter and endless fun.

Blind Man's Buff added an element of mystery as blindfolded players relied on their senses to move through the playful chaos.  In the circle of Ring-a-Ring-a-Roses, we danced and sang, our voices blending with the popular nursery rhyme.  Scattered toys, skipping ropes and hoops were strewn across the pavements inviting anyone to join in the laughter and play.  The tradition of swapping cigarette cards thrived, as we exchanged coveted collectable pictures with eagerness, learning (without realising it) the basics of worth, negotiation and compromise.  These enticing games were routes of expression, channels of friendship and sources of endless fun.  In the streets of the 1950s, childhood flourished in creativity, physical activity, and the pure magic of shared moments.

Even when I was engrossed in play, I never lost sight of Mam's instructions.  I knew that dinner would be waiting for me at 6:30pm sharp, and I made sure to obey. Evening approached and Susan would go indoors, drawn by the glow of the television screen.  However, television remained a luxury beyond Mam's reach.  Even the thought of renting one from the Rediffusion shop in Belgrave Gate was an impossibility.  We could only dream of such a luxury.

# Eleven

*T*he late summer of 1954 rolled around and with it, the progressing of a new chapter in my school life, moving into the junior classes.  Taylor Street School boasted a unique feature: a roof-top playground.  The prospect of playing on the roof, previously off-limits, was tremendously exciting.  Junior school also promised swimming lessons and nature studies at nearby Abbey Park, opportunities to explore and learn about the world around me.

I felt a twinge of apprehension at the prospect of having new classmates which meant forming new friendships, something I found both worrying and daunting at the same time.  Thankfully, my best friend, Carol, remained by my side, providing me with her friendly support.  Together, one by one, we managed the changes that were inevitable in our lives.

Visits from the school nurse were always a welcome interruption to the daily routine, though not without some anxiety for us.

With a variety of health checks taking place, the nit nurse's visits were perhaps the most dreaded.  With organised accuracy, she made her rounds, armed with a nit comb and a keen eye for infestations.  As the nurse entered the classroom, silence fell over us.  One by one, we lined up, nervously awaiting our turn for inspection. With gentle and thorough movements, the nurse combed through each child's hair, searching for any signs of the dreaded head lice.

The health checks didn't end there. Routine eye and hearing tests made sure that every child's senses were in proper working order. Even though they happened on a regular basis, the visits from the dentist were a constant source of both fear and relief. However, they were nothing short of a nightmare for me. The sound of the drill, the sterile smell of the treatment room, and the sensation of cotton wool being pushed into my mouth by unfamiliar hands filled me with dread. Despite the dentist's best efforts to reassure me, I couldn't shake off the anxiety that gripped me every time I sat in the dentist's chair. The experience was often painful and unsettling, leaving a lasting impression on my young mind.

As I grew older, I avoided dental appointments whenever possible, preferring to endure the occasional toothache rather than face the dreaded dentist's chair. It wasn't until much later in life that I realised the importance of regular dental care and overcame my fear through gentle, patient dentistry. Looking back, it becomes obvious that my early experiences with the school dentist had shaped my dread and apprehension.

We tend not to think about polio these days.  We have largely forgotten the awful effects of this disease that struck fear into the hearts of both parents and teachers alike.  An amazing thing happened during my childhood.  There was finally a glimmer of hope.  In 1954, an important breakthrough in the form of a polio vaccine was introduced and administered in schools.  This powerful vaccine brought a sense of overall relief, knowing that every child was now protected against the crippling disease that had once threatened communities.  The impact of the polio vaccine went far beyond individual families and school communities.  Worldwide vaccination almost eradicated polio, providing the way for a future free from its devastating grip.

As children lined up to receive their injection, there was a noticeable sense of expectancy and gratitude. Parents breathed a sigh of relief.

However, not all childhood diseases could be prevented through vaccination.  Measles, with its characteristic rash and high fever, could spread like wildfire, leaving a trail of sick children in its path. Mumps, with its tell-tale swelling just below the ears, could lead to complications such as meningitis or deafness if not treated.  Communities rallied together, offering support to those affected by outbreaks. Neighbours checked in on one another and shared information to help stop the spread of disease.

Class sizes in the 1950s and early 1960s swelled with the post-war baby boom, often exceeding 30 children in each class.  With no classroom assistants to help, discipline was maintained entirely by the class teacher.  Physical punishment was not uncommon, whether it be a rap with the ruler on the knuckles, buttocks, or palm of the student's hand.

I settled into my new class but found I was struggling.  In stark contrast to the warmth and creativity of my infant years, the teachers were stern and the lessons were colourless exercises on the blackboard.  Desperate to hold on to informality, I felt uneasy with my teacher's strict manner.  Anything I tried to do to connect with her was met with disapproval.

During school assembly one morning, my world was turned upside down.  Sitting cross-legged on the wooden block floor, I was picked out by the headmaster for my apparent wrong-doing: chewing gum.  Although I protested my innocence, I was dismissed from the assembly, my cheeks red, burning with embarrassment and confusion.

I made a brave decision, driven by a mixture of emotion and fear.  Leaving the confines of the school hall, I set off on my journey home, seeking help and understanding from my ever-supportive Nana.  My determination strengthened with each step, I was so upset and mad at the unfairness I had suffered.

I walked through the winding streets, my heart full of mixed emotions, finding relief in the knowledge that I would not be alone.  With Nana's gentle guidance and wisdom, I knew I would find the courage to face whatever lay ahead.  My footsteps carried me further from the school and closer to home, giving me a great sense of comfort.  As I entered my Nana's warm embrace, I expected understanding.

Instead, I was met with a serious telling off.

Nana was so angry at my foolish decision.  Concerned for my safety, she was shocked at my impulsive behaviour, pointing out the dangers of walking home alone.  My heart sank as I realised my mistake, my sense of independence overshadowed by the severity of my Nana's disappointment.

Just as I felt the weight of my actions bearing down on me, a glimmer of hope appeared in the form of Mrs Radley, our neighbour from next door.  She had seen me in the yard and popped her head around my Nana's door to check if everything was alright.  Sensing our upset, Mrs Radley offered a reassuring hand, willing to take me back to school and ensure my safe return.  With Mrs Radley's support, I felt a little less upset and thankful for the chance to make things right.  Walking back to school together, I found calm in Mrs Radley's company, my anxiety eased by her reassuring presence.

After school, I faced the consequences of my actions with a new point of view.  Though I had acted without thinking, I had learned a valuable lesson about the importance of safety and responsibility.

On Mam´s return home, my heart fluttered with a mix of apprehension and hope.  I knew that facing Mam´s reaction would be another hurdle to overcome, but I held on to the feeling that Mam would understand the reason behind my spontaneous action.

Mam stepped through the door and I braced myself for the inevitable conversation.  With my voice trembling, I explained the events that had taken place during morning assembly, pointing out my innocence in the matter of the chewing gum accusation.  Mam listened with a patient ear and, to my relief, her expression softening as she absorbed my words.  Though initially taken aback by my decision to walk home alone, Mam´s concern dissolved into understanding as I explained the reassurance given by Mrs Radley and the importance to seek comfort from my Nana.

Physical Education at school brought its own challenges.  I grappled with a mix of excitement and apprehension every three weeks when it was time for swimming lessons.  Due to the large class sizes, the school could only accommodate a few pupils at a time for swimming, resulting in lessons being spread out over three-week intervals.  This meant I had to wait for my turn, taking part in alternative activities like rounders, acrobatics, or dancing during the weeks in between.

Although I enjoyed the various activities at school, I felt unwilling to participate fully.  In those days, there was no designated gym kit for primary schools.  Instead, we were expected to remove our outer clothes and participate in PE in our vests, knickers, or underpants, often accompanied by bare feet or cheap plimsolls bought from Woolworths.

The prospect of revealing my body in such a public setting was daunting.  I couldn't shake off the fear of being made fun of or judged by my peers.  Each PE session became a battleground between my desire to take part and my fear of being mocked.  Standing beside my classmates in my navy knickers and bare feet, I kept my embarrassment hidden, not wanting to bother anyone with my insecurities.  It was some time before I realised that my worth was not measured by my appearance but by the strength of my spirit.

However, my growing withdrawal didn't go unnoticed by Mam.  Concerned about my well-being, she decided to take action.  With the help of her parents, Nana and Grandad, who contributed towards the cost, Mam enrolled me into the nearby Vestry Street Swimming Baths, giving me the opportunity to have swimming lessons once a week.

The prospect of weekly swimming lessons was just wonderful!  Not only did I love the water and the feeling of weightlessness it brought, but it also meant I could indulge in a thorough soak in the baths provided at the facility.  A visit to Vestry Street became more than just swimming lessons; it turned into happy moments for Mam and me to enjoy a relaxing soak in the public baths, washing away not only physical dirt but also the weight of my worries and insecurities.

With each swimming lesson, my abilities and confidence grew, mastering various strokes and even learning how to dive gracefully into the pool.  My dedication and perseverance paid off, and soon I found myself outshining my peers in the water.  The feeling of being ahead of my classmates brought me a sense of pride and accomplishment.  During school swimming sessions I enjoyed the opportunity to show off my skills, effortlessly gliding through the water while my classmates were struggling to keep up.

Practising at the Vestry Street Swimming Baths for over a year, I completed my formal lessons.  However, my love for swimming only deepened.  I was determined to maintain my most recently taught skills and get even better, making it a point to visit the pool at least once a week after school.  I continued my solo swimming sessions and my confidence soared to new heights.  My once-hidden insecurities faded away, replaced by a self-assurance that was impossible to ignore.  Whether I was diving into the water or effortlessly gliding across the pool, my new-found confidence was apparent to all who knew me.

On a sunny Saturday afternoon, while playing with the local kids, I overheard them discussing Sunday school.  Initially unsure, I showed disinterest, blaming my dislike of regular school.  However, my curiosity got the better of me as they described Sunday school as a place with kind teachers, beautiful songs, and fascinating stories about Jesus.

Intrigued by the chance of a different kind of learning experience, I decided to give Sunday school a try.  I dashed home to seek Mam's permission and approval.  Breathless with excitement, I exclaimed,

"Mammy, Mammy, can I go to Sunday School tomorrow?"  Listening attentively, Mam offered a cautious response.

"Are you sure you want to go, darling?"  My enthusiasm was out of control as I reassured her with an emphatic,

"Oh yes, please, Mammy!"

Seeing the spark in my eyes, Mam asked about the church I would be going to.  I explained that it was a Baptist chapel called Carley Street, where some of the neighbourhood kids attended.  Curious to learn more, Mam reached out for information from Dottie next door, knowing she was familiar with the chapel.

After gathering information and ensuring the arrangements were suitable, Mam gave me the green light to attend Sunday school with Dottie's two boys.  I was filled with excitement.  It was as if I was beginning a new journey of exploration and discovery while I eagerly looked forward to my first Sunday school experience, ready to embrace the new opportunities that lay ahead.

Just after lunch, Roger and Roy, the boys from next door, arrived to collect me.  Together, we made our way to the Baptist chapel, situated just down Wharf Street, at the corner of Carley Street.  I learned that the chapel, now occupying its new building, had been relocated from Wheat Street due to a demolition order.

I was warmly introduced by the boys and welcomed by my two teachers.  The Sunday school classroom buzzed with a dozen or more children, some I recognised and some new.  Although I had been nervous initially, I felt embraced by my peers who eagerly invited me to join them.

One of the teachers, Miss Jane, stood out.  Over time, we developed a close bond with Miss Jane offering support during a particularly difficult period in my life.

The two-hour class flew by as we listened to stories about Jesus and sang gentle hymns.  I was captivated by the experience, surprised at how quickly the time passed.

Before going home, Miss Jane presented me with a small book of stories about Jesus and a bookmark, tokens of my time at Sunday School.  I treasured these gifts; they reminded me of the warmth and kindness I had been shown on my first visit.  Already looking forward to the next Sunday, I left with a heart full of joyfulness.

I was brimming with excitement to share my Sunday School experience with Mam.  Rushing through the door, I shouted,

"Mammy, you won't believe what happened today!"  I eagerly explained about meeting a kind lady named Miss Jane who was far nicer than any of my school teachers.  My excitement was apparent as I started singing a song I had learned, repeating it over and over again, my enthusiasm infectious.  I dashed into Nana's room, continuing to sing.

Curious about the book and bookmark that I had brought home, Mam gently questioned me.

"Anna, should you have brought these things home? You must return them when you go to Sunday School again." Without missing a beat, I assured Mam,

"Mammy, Miss Jane gave them to me because I started Sunday School.  All the new children receive these gifts."  Relieved, Mam nodded, saying,

"Oh, that's alright then.  I just wanted to be sure you hadn't taken them without permission."

My growing confidence was obvious in my eagerness to excel in everything I tried.  Whether it was swimming or aiming to be the top student in my class, I approached every challenge with determination.  When I heard about Sunday School, I didn't hesitate to join in.  In fact, I welcomed it wholeheartedly.  With each new experience, I was blossoming, growing up beside laughter and a sense of belonging among my friends.  I displayed a willingness to try anything.  Undeterred by fear or uncertainty, I was truly ready to take on the world.

# Twelve

*M*y childhood was marked by frequent battles with tonsillitis, particularly during the harsh winter months. Despite Mam's efforts to seek medical help, the doctor's remedies seemed worthless, offering nothing more than antibiotics and fever powders.  The recurring illness not only affected my health but also cast a shadow over the family, especially when Nana fell ill due to colds, often resulting in bronchitis or pneumonia and hospitalisation. The fear and anxiety that gripped the family during Nana's hospital stays was overwhelming, leaving me upset and worried.  Despite everyone's attempts to prevent spreading their colds to Nana, it seemed inevitable in the close quarters of our home.

My tonsillitis worsened with each episode, my doctor finally recommending a tonsillectomy, together with the removal of my adenoids.  At eight years old, and with understandable apprehension about the operation, my anxiety was magnified by the thought of being away from home.  Despite my fears, Mam felt a sense of relief knowing that something would finally be done to address my health issues, especially since my schooling had begun to suffer.

On the morning of my operation, Mam and I made our way to the Clarendon Park Children's Clinic, arriving promptly at 8am.  Having fasted since the previous night, I was hungry and nervous, but determined to face the surgery ahead.  However, the separation from Mam was a difficult moment for both of us.  She reluctantly left me in the care of the nurses, trusting that I would be in good hands.

Inside the clinic, I found support in the company of other children facing similar procedures.  Though initially distraught by our parents' absence, we soon supported each other through our shared experience. The clinic became a temporary home for us all as we prepared for and recovered from our surgeries.

Mam's days were filled with worry and longing to be with me.  In spite of the financial strain of leaving work early to visit me, her concerns were focused solely on my well-being.  Fortunately, the convenient location allowed Mam to catch a bus from Humberstone Gate directly to the clinic, easing some of the logistical challenges.  Mam counted down the hours until visiting time, eagerly anticipating the chance to see me and reassure herself of my progress.  Money for the bus fares mattered little in comparison to the health and happiness of her little girl.

I found a small silver lining to the nerves and discomfort of my upcoming operation: the prospect of indulging in ice cream on the first day and then jelly and ice cream in the following days.  As I lay in my hospital bed, the thought of the cold, soothing treats was a moderate reward for the discomfort.

My operation went smoothly, and I returned to the ward feeling groggy from the anaesthetic. Mam arrived just as I began to stir from my drowsiness, her presence being a vital comfort to me in the strange hospital surroundings. Shortly after, it was time for us to have our tea, and to my delight, it was ice cream. Mam watched with a smile as I eagerly dug into my treat, knowing that the coldness would bring some relief to the soreness in my throat. Carefully, Mam helped me with my tea, relieved that my surgery had gone well and that I was on the road to recovery.

Due to my persistent high temperature and lingering lethargy, my stay at the clinic extended for two more days. Despite the discomfort and the desire to return home, I understood the need for further treatment and rest. As the weekend approached, the clinic closed its doors and I was transferred to Roecliffe Manor in Woodhouse Eaves, a picturesque village situated in the heart of the Charnwood Forest in Leicestershire.

Purchased by Leicestershire County Council in the 1940s, this stately mansion underwent a transformation. Once a grand estate, Roecliffe Manor was converted to a convalescent home for children recovering from various ailments. Many of the residents had battled common childhood illnesses of the time, such as pneumonia, diphtheria, or scarlet fever, while others, like me, had undergone surgeries, including tonsillectomies.

As I prepared for my transfer to Roecliffe Manor, I felt a mix of emotions.  While part of me longed for the familiarity of home, I also felt a touch of excitement at the thought of staying in the convalescent home, especially since it was situated near the woods.  I was pleased with the idea of being surrounded by nature during my recovery so I began the next phase of my journey to wellness, trusting that Roecliffe Manor would provide the care I needed to recover fully and return home healthy and happy.

Visiting me at Roecliffe Manor posed a transport nightmare for Mam, with the distance of 8 miles making it difficult to visit at the weekend.  However, my godparents, Auntie Glenis and Uncle John, recognised the value of family support during my recovery. Determined to ensure Mam could visit, Auntie Glenis and Uncle John made a special trip to Leicester to pick Mam up.

My stay at the convalescent home stretched on for what felt like an eternity.  My discontentment grew with each day that passed by, heightened by the small inconveniences and restrictions that annoyed me.  I hated the tin cup into which my drinks were poured and the tin plates that accompanied my meals, causing me to long for home even more.  The regimented walks every morning, conducted in single file, felt stifling.  Gone were the leisurely strolls where I could walk side by side with my friends, chatting and laughing freely.  Instead, I was confined to the structured routine of the convalescent home, longing for the spontaneity of life beyond its boundary.  Even the dormitory, shared with eleven other girls, became a source of annoyance for me. While I valued the friendships I had formed, the close quarters and varying personalities made for a challenging living arrangement.

But above all, it was the separation from Mam that weighed heaviest.  Despite the care and attention that I received from the staff and the friendship of my peers, nothing could replace Mam's warmth and love.

Finally, the day arrived when my time at the convalescent home came to an end.  Uncle John's car pulled into the driveway and my heart soared with relief and pleasure.  Thankful, I waved goodbye to the home that had been my temporary retreat, jumping with joy at the prospect of returning to the comfort of home.

# Thirteen

*A*s the year passed, I was increasingly drawn to lonely adventures in the war-torn wastelands of my imagination. While I once loved to play games of make-believe with my friends, I gradually became more of an outsider. School continued to hold little appeal for me, and although I applied effort in my studies, my interest dwindled with each passing day. Academic subjects only held my attention when I felt confident I wouldn't fall behind my classmates. My struggles with schoolwork mounted and so too did my difficulties in forming relationships with my peers. I was drifting, unable to bridge the gap between myself and the neighbourhood children who once filled my days with laughter and excitement.

In spite of this, there remained one bright spot in my world: the school roof. Whether attending summer lessons, posing for my school photograph, or simply basking in the freedom of playtime, the rooftop became a significant place for me. It was more than just a vantage point; it was an adventure waiting to happen, a place where I could escape the pressures of my daily life.

Although time on the school roof brought me immense pleasure, it also caused me pain. I loved having friends, playing rounders, and all the games

children played in the school playground.  But having
friends felt like a button waiting to be pressed, releasing
a storm I had to fight my way through.

My so-called 'friends' could be spiteful and hurtful.
They joined together to say nasty things when play
suddenly turned into friction.  They would argue with me
and, to get even, they would scream,

"Your Dad left you because he didn't want you,
and your Mam had to keep you because nobody else
wanted you either."  They also called me a 'bastard', a
word I neither knew nor understood, but I knew it wasn't
nice so I never told Mam.

With an immediate angry response, and without
thinking, I would shout,

"My daddy is dead! It's not fair, I hate you all!"
Then I would retire to sit alone on the playground
bench, and sob.  Was this one of the reasons I preferred
not to make friends, and why I only trusted Carol?  Carol
was different; she would never purposely hurt me.

Although I never allowed anyone to say nasty things
about Mam, I inwardly blamed her for causing me all
this anger, even though I had no idea of the truth nor of
the reason why.  The confusion and hurt felt like a
constant shadow, and despite the joy of the games, the
playground often became a battlefield of emotions that
I didn't fully understand.

One thing remained the same through it all: my unchanging friendship with Carol.  We forged a firm relationship together, finding contentment in each other's company amid the complexities of moving towards adolescence.  In a world where I felt increasingly isolated, Carol's presence was a comforting reassurance, a reminder that I was never truly alone.

During parents' evening that year, Mam sat across from my teacher, listening intently as concerns were raised about my lack of interest in my studies and my growing sense of apprehension about falling behind my peers.  She couldn't bear the thought of me feeling lost and alone, struggling to find my place in the world.  As the discussion continued, Mam's own observations echoed the teacher's words.  I had indeed become increasingly withdrawn.  It was a troubling realisation, one that compelled Mam to act.

Determined to uncover the source of my troubles, Mam chose to have a heart-to-heart conversation with me.  Sitting down beside me one evening, she gently broached the subject, her words edged with concern and love.

"What´s up, sweetheart?  There´s something bothering you, I know there is," Mam began, her voice soft and reassuring.  "Is there anything on your mind, anything worrying you?"

I hesitated at first, my eyes fixed on the floor as I battled with my thoughts.  But gradually, the floodgates opened, and I poured out my fears and frustrations to Mam.  I spoke of my struggles at school, my growing sense of isolation, and my longing to find my place in the world.  As my thoughts churned in my mind, a flood of emotions washed over me, changing my initial response into one of contempt.  Anger simmered beneath the surface as I confronted Mam with a barrage of questions, my voice trembling with pent-up resentment.

"Mam," I began, my tone tinged with accusation. "Where is my Daddy?  Everyone has a daddy except me."  My words were marked by the rawness of my emotions.  My heartache spilled over, each question a painful reminder of my longing for a family I felt was incomplete.

"Why don't I have a brother or sister?" I demanded, my voice overwhelmed with torment.  The tears flowed freely now, and I clung to the hope that Mam held the answers to my burning questions.  Deep down, I already sensed the truth I was unwilling to accept; the stark reality of my circumstances.

The conversation escalated, my desperation mounted and my cries growing louder with each passing moment. In my heartache, I lashed out, spitting hurtful words at the one person I loved most in the world.

"I love my Nana better than you," I spat, the words dripping with venom.  "And I wish I had a dad and not a mam."

The impact of my words echoed through the room, piercing Mam's heart like a knife.  The pain was evident, cutting deep into the core of her being.  Yet, through the anguish, a flicker of understanding emerged; a realisation that my outburst stemmed from a place of deep-seated hurt and longing.  In that moment of reckoning, we found strength in each other's grasp, together in our journey toward healing and forgiveness.

In the wake of our turbulent discussion, the days that followed felt heavy with tension for us both.  The wounds of our exchange lingered, casting a shadow over our once serene household.  Throughout the turmoil, Nana was our mutual support.

Nana became a shelter for me with her gentle words and a comforting presence, offering a listening ear and a shoulder to lean on in my time of need.  In the warmth of her cuddles, I started to open up in ways I never thought possible, sharing my fears, frustrations, and dreams with a new sense of vulnerability.  I began to confront the harsh realities of my situation, slowly but surely coming to terms with the absence of a father and the complexities of my family dynamic.

The following weeks witnessed a sense of peace descending upon the household, guided by the love and support that flowed freely between three generations. With Nana's guidance and Mam's dedicated presence, I began my journey of self-discovery, finding strength in my vulnerability and courage in my acceptance.

Despite life returning to some resemblance of normality, the confrontation had certainly worried Mam more than I realised. To try to address my need for a father figure, she arranged a surprise.

One sunny morning, Uncle Edward, clad in his green uniform, proposed an unconventional outing for me. Despite it not being standard protocol, he decided to take me along on one of his work trips to the garages delivering supplies for a petrol company. My eyes sparkled with excitement as I climbed into the cab of Uncle Edward's massive petrol tanker, feeling a surge of importance as I sat beside him. The noise of the engine beneath us was thrilling as we set off on our journey through Leicester.

I watched in admiration as Uncle Edward expertly climbed onto the top of the tanker, his heavy gloves gripping the ladder with ease. I was fascinated to see how he attached the hose for the petrol to pour through, absorbing every detail of the process.

Beyond the technicalities of his job, I loved the precious moments spent together the most.  Continuing through the city streets, Uncle Edward and I shared stories, laughter, and quiet reflection, creating a friendship that went beyond words.

Returning home, I carried with me the memories of our day out, a treasure trove of moments that I would hold dear for years to come.  And though the longing for a father figure still remained, I was happy in the knowledge that I was surrounded by a family who cherished me unconditionally.

One day, the family gathered for a discussion and Mam proposed the idea of a family outing, suggesting that Nana and Grandad, Nana's health being fairly stable, should join in.  With a little extra care, she believed we could all enjoy a day out together.  Encouraged by the idea, Mam ventured to a shop in Humberstone Gate to purchase tickets for the excursion.  She was presented with various options for day trips.  While the mystery trip stirred her curiosity, she finally decided on a day trip to Llangollen in Wales.  She knew the prospect of going to another country would fill me with excitement, even though Wales wasn't too far away.  With enthusiasm, she booked four tickets, using the money I had raised from my 'Penny for the Guy' initiative, fulfilling her promise to do something special for the family with the money.

The day of our adventure dawned.  The weather
proved to be perfect, a promising sign for the outing.  We
set off on our journey, filled with excitement and quickly
connecting with the other day-trippers on the coach.
There was always one who kept us laughing with silly
jokes, another who led the singing and another who took
a cap round, collecting tips for the very obliging and
likeable driver.  As we drove through picturesque
countryside, laughter and conversation filled the air,
creating memories that would be cherished for years to
come.

We arrived in Llangollen, greeted by the sight of
quaint streets lined with charming shops and busy cafes.
The day stretched before us like an open road, beckoning
us to explore and discover all that this charming town
had to offer.  Together, we explored, admiring the
historical centre and the glimpses of Welsh culture.  We
appreciated our scenic walk along the River Dee and
enjoyed a ride on the historic Llangollen Railway.

As the sun began to set on our day, we gathered for a
final meal, a picnic prepared by Mam.  We then started
our journey home after a delightful and happy day out.
My excitement gave way to discomfort as I began to feel
queasy.  As miles passed, my nausea intensified, until I
could bear it no longer.  Concerned for me, Mam
approached the bus driver, requesting a brief stop to
allow me some fresh air.  This wasn't the first time I had

experienced travel sickness, despite Mam's efforts to alleviate my symptoms with Kwells sickness tablets. Although popular, they seemed ineffective in combating my persistent problem.  It wasn't until a chance conversation with a colleague that Mam stumbled upon a simple yet effective solution.  Her colleague suggested sitting me on a newspaper during bus journeys, claiming it would help prevent me from feeling sick.

With nothing to lose, Mam was willing to give it a try.  On boarding the coach on another trip to the seaside, she placed me on a folded newspaper, hoping against hope that this unconventional remedy would prove successful.  To her amazement, it did.  I remained free from sickness for the duration of the journey.  From that day forward, I never suffered from travel sickness again. Whether it was the placebo effect or a stroke of luck, the simple act of sitting on a newspaper seemed to work wonders for me.  The sight of me comfortably and happily perched on a newspaper during bus rides became a familiar sight: a small price to pay for the peace of mind it brought to the two of us.

# Fourteen

*I* had always been a somewhat independent child, preferring to tackle challenges on my own.  Whether it was helping Mam with chores around the house or exploring the neighbourhood with friends, I began to discover my own strengths and talents.

In the centre of Lee Street was Lee Circle, a sprawling expanse of flat land steeped in history.  This was where my Uncle Edward had taught me how to ride my bike and it held a special place in my heart.  This busy circular hub had emerged from the remnants of demolished buildings, its vast circumference connecting numerous roads and junctions.

One of the many roads leading from Lee Circle was Charles Street, a thoroughfare alive with the rhythm of urban life.  Along this busy stretch of road stood a landmark of distinction: The Horse Repository Hotel.  This establishment was steeped in tradition and charm.  It was a haven for travellers and equestrian enthusiasts alike.  But what truly set The Horse Repository Hotel apart was not just its inviting exterior or cosy rooms.  Tucked away at the rear of the building lay the Horse Repository itself, a hidden treasure awaiting discovery by those with an affection for horses and business.

The repository was a marvel in its own right, boasting a spacious parade ring where horses and hounds alike were paraded with grace and poise.  Buyers and sellers would assemble here, their voices mingling with the clip-clop of hooves as deals were struck and dreams exchanged hands.

Lee Circle became an integral part of my life as I walked around it, my steps guided by the charm of the famous Horse Repository.  Though my visits were limited to school holidays, I eagerly looked forward to the sight of horse boxes parked on the waste ground that formed the circle's centre.

With each visit, my fascination with the repository grew.  I would strike up conversations with the owners of the horse boxes, my curiosity heightened by the activity that surrounded them.  I watched intently, absorbing every detail with wide-eyed wonder as they unloaded their horses and prepared to lead them to the repository for sale.

Over time, I became a familiar face at the repository, my presence welcomed by the owners and vendors alike. And then, one day, my persistence paid off.  A kind-hearted owner, recognising my enthusiasm, offered me the chance to parade a horse around the ring, hoping to catch the eye of potential buyers.  Ecstatic at the opportunity, I didn't hesitate.  With a heart full of pride, I strutted around the ring, leading the majestic creature with a sense of importance contradicting my young age. For a brief moment, I was transformed, a queen of the ring, commanding attention and admiration with every step.

At the Horse Repository, all manner of horses and hounds went under the hammer, from sturdy carriage horses to sleek hunters.  Despite alterations and closures due to wartime necessities, it remained a cornerstone of the community, closing its doors for the last time in the 1960s.

I loved my moments of solitude, but I was now more willing to step out of my comfort zone and embrace the world around me.  Though life was changing, one thing remained constant: the love and stability of our home in Crafton Street.

Across the shared communal yard of Crafton Street, lived the Radley family.  Their back door, always left ajar like a welcome sign, mirrored my own, inviting me into their world with open arms.  Mrs. Radley, known affectionately as Dottie to me, became a familiar presence in my life.

Bernard Radley, Dottie's husband, cut a striking figure with his towering frame and his handsome features.  He toiled away at the local gas works on the aptly named Gas Street, providing for his family while

Dottie tended to their four lively boys: Reuben, Ronald, Roger, and Roy.

Despite the friendship shared in the communal space, there were moments of discord. The boys, engrossed in their games, occasionally shunned my company, dismissing me with a wave of exclusion. These episodes stirred tension and misunderstandings, often requiring the intervention of our mothers to restore peace. Even with the occasional clashes, the bonds of neighbourly affection endured.

Mam found herself absorbed in her own responsibilities, leaving little room for socialising with Dottie. Her long hours at work and the demands of household chores and care giving for Nana left her with little energy for social calls. Nonetheless, the shared experiences of communal living fostered a sense of unity among the close neighbours.

Though the interactions between Mam and Dottie were infrequent, the spirit of community prevailed. They rallied around each other in moments of need, offering support and understanding. In the ebb and flow of life on Crafton Street, with the laughter of children and the hum of daily routines, the ties that bound Mam and I and the Radley family grew stronger. The yard, sometimes a battleground of childhood squabbles, was proof of the enduring neighbourly ties, where disagreements were soon forgotten, and harmony easily restored.

Living in the close quarters of the communal space had its drawbacks, with privacy being a precious commodity in short supply.  The houses, mere reflections of each other, lacked certain modern conveniences such as bathrooms which meant that children were bathed in the kitchen sink most evenings.  Hot water was provided by heating several saucepans on the stove.  The lack of privacy extended beyond the absence of a bathroom.  With no curtains at the kitchen window, Mam improvised with an old sheet to shield me from prying eyes.  As I grew older, I rebelled against this makeshift barrier, craving a feeling of autonomy and privacy.

Another source of discomfort was the outdoor toilet, a small lean-to attached to the kitchen wall.  At night, the darkness inside was broken only by the feeble glow of the moonlight filtering through the cracks of the wooden door.  The chain for flushing hung precariously high, beyond my reach, adding to my sense of unease.  Instead of toilet paper, squares of newspaper on a string served as a simple substitute, a reminder of the modesty of our circumstances.

However, it wasn't the lack of cleanliness that haunted me the most about the amenities.  It was the presence of spiders.  A childhood encounter with a spider had left an unforgettable memory.  One day, I reached into the cupboard to retrieve my wellington boots and a spider darted up my sleeve, sending shivers of terror down my spine.  From that moment on, I lived in constant fear of encountering them again.  In the dimly lit confines of the outside toilet, unsettling shadows danced on the walls, and the silence was punctuated by the occasional scuttle of tiny legs.  Every corner held the potential for a terrifying encounter, a reminder of the vulnerability that came with communal living.

The expectation of a new addition to the Radley family brought excitement and joy.  As Dottie's pregnancy progressed, the whispers of anticipation filled the air.

"I bet you want a girl this time!" became a common refrain, echoing the collective desire for a daughter to balance the brood of boys.  Dottie's response, filled with maternal love and dedicated affection, affirmed that her heart would overflow with love for her new arrival regardless of the gender.

In early June of 1957, the long-awaited moment arrived and a beautiful baby girl entered the world. Dottie and Bernard named her Frances, a name filled with promises of sweetness and light.

The arrival of little Frances brought a renewed sense of purpose and joy.  I eagerly took on the role of doting helper, relishing the opportunity to care for the new-

born.  Whether it was accompanying Dottie on walks
with the pram or assisting with feeding, I thoroughly
enjoyed involving myself with the newest member of the
Radley family.

I couldn't help but wonder, though, about the choice
of name.  Why Frances?  And why not follow the family
tradition of starting the name with an 'R', like Rose,
Rita, Ruby or Rachel?  I never did get an answer.  But in
the end, the name mattered little, and it certainly wasn't
anything to do with me!  What truly mattered was the
love and happiness that little Frances brought into their
lives, a precious light in the shared journey of communal
living.  I knew that no matter what name she had,
Frances would be cherished beyond measure by her
family and community alike.

# Fifteen

*M*y childhood memories sparkle with recollections of seaside outings with Mam.  The salty breeze, the rhythmic sound of crashing waves, the sand that got into everything, huge ice-creams, sugary minty sticks of rock and long strolls along the prom were familiar things in my young life.  I had never ventured away from home without Mam by my side, except for that one time, when my tonsils had to be removed, but that had hardly been a holiday.  The idea of being away from Mam for an extended period was both daunting and exciting.

Along the coast of Mablethorpe stood the Leicester Children's Holiday Home, a place of happiness and good times for underprivileged children from Leicestershire. Established in 1937, it had become a home for countless youngsters, offering them the chance to experience the wonders of a seaside holiday.  Each summer, hundreds of children from the city centre would bid farewell to their families and embark on a journey to the coast.  It was, for many, their first taste of freedom, their first opportunity to explore beyond the confines of their urban surroundings.

I had never experienced a full week's holiday before. When my name was suggested for a nomination to attend the Leicester Children's Holiday Home during a school parents' evening, Mam eagerly agreed.  The prospect of experiencing the magic of the seaside made me more than happy so I hopped around with excitement when I saw the letter confirming my selection in the post.  On the day of departure, I stood at the bus stop in Charles Street, my suitcase packed to the brim with anticipation.  I clasped Mam´s hand with a mixture of nerves and excitement as I watched the bus approach, ready to whisk me away on my seaside adventure.  I boarded the bus alongside other eager children, secretly placed a newspaper on my seat and waved goodbye to Mam, blowing her a kiss from the window as the bus pulled away.

Underneath the clear skies of Mablethorpe, away from city life, my feet found their way to the dance floor. But it wasn't rock 'n' roll or modern dance that captured my heart.  No, it was the elegant and timeless waltz that caught my attention and delighted my spirit.  Guided by patient instructors and encouraged by a new group of friends, I immersed myself in the graceful movements of the dance.  With each step, I felt a sense of freedom, as if the rhythm of the music mirrored the beat of my own heart.  Every evening, I twirled and spun, lost in the magic of the moment.  Through the simple and profound act of dancing, I felt a sense of connection: connection to my fellow dancers, to the music, and to the beauty of the seaside surroundings.  In those moments of movement and expression, I discovered a part of myself I hadn't known before: a spirit of rhythm that danced freely beneath the summer skies of Mablethorpe.

Although dancing was a massive highlight of my holiday in Mablethorpe, the seven days were full of fun. The home was near the beach, and the sand dunes were within easy reach. We visited the dunes every day and were allowed to play freely, transforming the area into a magical wonderland. We played Hide-and-seek, imagined ourselves as pirates, and played games of Blind Man´s Buff.

Swimming was another highlight, though we were not allowed to swim in the sea. Instead, we paddled and splashed about, drenching everyone in our path. The laughter and joy in those moments were infectious. One special occasion that stands out was the visit to a beach-side café for tea. We had sausage, chips and beans. I felt like I was in another world. For the first time, I felt relaxed around the friends I had made, feeling happy, forgetting my need for Mam to be around.

Mablethorpe had been wonderful but a week away from home had been enough and I was glad when the bus rolled back into Charles Street, Leicester. I could see Mam through the dusty windows, a familiar figure in the distance, waving eagerly. After days of seaside adventures and newfound independence, the sight of her filled me with a sense of welcoming and warmth.

Stepping off the bus, I experienced a moment unlike any other. I had always clung close to Mam in the past, seeking security in her embrace. But now, as I returned to Mam´s welcoming hug, there was a newfound sense of independence and confidence in my appearance. Witnessing her daughter's display of autonomy filled Mam with pride and reassurance. We made our way home, walking side by side and, in that moment, my journey towards independence took a significant step forward.

My passion for ballroom dancing filled every corner of the house with joy and energy. From room to room, I would waltz gracefully, my movements fluid and my spirit soaring. I begged Mam to watch me, my eyes alight with excitement and enthusiasm. I would hum a lively tune, gliding effortlessly around the house, lost in the magic of the dance. Mam couldn't help but laugh as she watched me twirl and spin, loving the sight of my happiness.

Sensing my deep love for dance and seeing how much it meant to me, Mam suggested dancing lessons. Despite the financial strain, she was determined to support my passion and enhance my zest for life. She knew she had to find a way to make it happen. She reached out to local dance studios, enquiring about class schedules and fees, looking for a suitable opportunity for me to pursue my dreams. Finally, after much searching, she found a dance studio that offered affordable lessons. She enrolled me in the classes, knowing that it would be a wonderful opportunity for me to explore my passion for dance and cultivate my talents. And so, I eagerly looked forward to my first dance lesson at the Bernard and Muriel Stanger Embassy Dance School in the Secular Hall in Humberstone Gate.

Mam couldn't help but marvel at the transformation she had witnessed in me. From the carefree waltzes around the house to the determination to pursue my dreams, my love for dancing had become a shining example of joy and inspiration in our lives.

# Sixteen

*I* was astonished and excited as I unwrapped my first pair of silver dance shoes, a thoughtful gift from my Auntie Glenis and Uncle John. With their shimmering elegance, the shoes seemed to hold the promise of countless twirls and spins on the dance floor. Little did I know that these shoes would be the first of many treasures bestowed upon me by my Auntie Glenis who would play an integral role in shaping my journey through the world of dance. From stitching exquisite dresses for competitions and examinations to offering support and encouragement, Auntie Glenis became my faithful companion in my dance experiences.

My silver shoes sparkled in the sunlight as I walked for the first time to the dance school. I was greeted by Bernard, the co-owner of the school, along with his wife Muriel. Their warm smiles and welcoming personalities instantly put me at ease, washing away any nerves I may have felt. Thrilled, I eagerly began my lessons, starting with the timeless waltz. Under Bernard's patient guidance, I danced the steps with grace and precision, my heart swelling with pride at each movement mastered and the music making my heart sing.

Despite being a beginner, I approached my lessons with a confidence and enthusiasm that belied my lack of experience.  Like a duck to water, I embraced my passion, immersing myself fully in the rhythms and movements that filled me with joy.  Dancing across the studio floor, my silver shoes sparkling with each step, I knew that I had found a place where I belonged.  With Auntie Glenis by my side, cheering me on every step of the way, my journey through the world of dance was just beginning.

This love for dancing opened the door to a world of music, where rhythm and melody intertwined to create a symphony of sound and movement.  As I delved deeper into the world of dance, mastering the steps of the waltz, foxtrot, tango, and quickstep, I also found myself captivated by the diverse sounds that accompanied each one.  My appreciation for music blossomed with each new dance I learned.  The graceful melodies of the waltz stirred something within me, evoking feelings of elegance and romance.  The lively tempo of the foxtrot filled me with intoxicating energy, while the sultry notes of the tango (in those days classed as ballroom) ignited a passion deep within my soul.  And as I glided across the dance floor to the brisk rhythm of the quickstep, I felt a sense of freedom and exhilaration unlike any other.

But it wasn't just the classical tunes that captured my heart.  Through my exploration of dance, I also discovered the electrifying world of Rock 'n' Roll.  The pulsating beats and infectious rhythms of artists like

Elvis Presley and Little Richard brought a new dimension to my musical palette, opening my ears to the sounds of modern-day music. With each twist and turn on the dance floor, I was swept away by the music, losing myself in its melodies and rhythms. Whether I was swaying to the gentle strains of a waltz or shaking my hips to the lively beats of Rock 'n' Roll, music became an integral part of my life.

Within a year, Bernard saw my potential and enrolled me in my first exam: the coveted bronze medal. Auntie Glenis, ever supportive, crafted a stunning pink dress fit for a queen, reflecting my grace and elegance on the dance floor.

On Saturday, 23rd February 1957, Mam, Auntie Glenis and I made our way to the dance studio. Despite the magnitude of the occasion, I radiated confidence and determination, my nerves masked by excitement and readiness to showcase my skills to the world.

The music filled the air and the judges took their places. Bernard and I danced gracefully through the four required dances, our movements a testament to months of dedication and hard work. With each step, my passion and talent shone brightly, captivating the audience and leaving the judges impressed. My heart swelled with pride as I danced, knowing that Mam and Auntie Glenis were watching and as the final notes of the music faded away, my smile radiated with the joy of accomplishment.

At the next dance session, amid cheers and applause from my fellow dancers, I was awarded my first dance medal, a shining reward for my dedication and talent. The ceremony was a special moment, a celebration of my journey and the beginning of many more triumphs to come. The bronze medal in my hands was more than a medal; it was proof of my perseverance, and the unrelenting support of my loved ones. I was proud of myself.

My passion for dance continued to flourish as I dedicated myself to my training at the studio over the years. I honed my skills and pushed myself to new heights, guided by the patient instruction of Bernard and encouraged by my own determination to excel. As the years went by, my dedication paid off, culminating in a string of impressive achievements. I proudly earned my silver and gold medals in ballroom dancing. And it didn't stop there. Driven by my thirst for excellence, I dived into the intricate world of Latin American dances, mastering the Cha-cha-cha, the Samba, Rock 'n' Roll, and the Rumba with finesse and grace. My passion for these vibrant and rhythmic dances earned me the prestigious first Gold Bar, a mark of distinction in the dance community.

Auntie Glenis remained a permanent source of support and encouragement throughout, ensuring that I looked as beautiful as I danced. With her skilful hands and keen eye for design, Auntie Glenis crafted stunning costumes that not only complemented my performances but also enhanced my natural grace and elegance. Standing on the dance floor, adorned in her creations, I felt confident and elated. Each twirl and each spin were proof of the years of hard work and dedication I had poured into my craft. And as I danced, I was living my dream.

There was one bittersweet aspect to my success: the absence of my beloved Nana. She was no longer able to leave her bed, requiring constant care and relying on oxygen to sustain her throughout the day.

Whenever I visited Nana, I would eagerly twirl and glide around the foot of her bed, my graceful movements bringing a spark of joy to her eyes. I shared the intricacies of my life with dance, recounting my achievements and the challenges I had overcome along the way. Despite the physical limitations that confined her to her bed, Nana remained a pillar of strength and inspiration. As I danced for her, I cherished every moment spent in her presence, knowing that our bond transcended physical distance and limitations.

Although Mam loved dancing, she didn't share my passion. I embraced it whole-heartedly. This love of movement and rhythm wasn't a fleeting hobby; it became an integral part of my identity, one that I proudly see reflected in my family today.

My daughter, Gemma, inherited this passion for music and dance.  Her love for the art is palpable, and she never misses the opportunity to be the first on the dance floor, no matter what the occasion.  Gemma´s spirited energy and infectious enthusiasm for dance light up any room.  This family tradition has also been inherited by my two eldest granddaughters, Maria and Kate.

Kate, in particular, has taken this familial love for dance to extraordinary heights.  She delved deeply into the science of dance, mastering its techniques and intricacies.  Her dedication and talent led her to become the director of her own dance school, a place where creativity and discipline blend seamlessly.  Kate´s productions are credit to her skill and passion, often featuring the bright talents of her sister, Maria, and her Auntie Gemma.  Their artistry not only showcases their individual talents but also symbolises the enduring legacy of dance in our family.  Through every pirouette, every leap, and every synchronised step, they celebrate the joy and unity that music and dance have brought into their lives.

I am happy and proud of this and I know Mam would have been too.

## Seventeen

*L*ife in our house had always been filled with warmth and love, despite the occasional bumps in the road.  Now at the age of 10, I had known little disruption in my daily routine.  There were moments of upset, occasional arguments, and the ever-present worry of financial strain but the family remained steady through it all.

New Year's Day, 1958, had dawned upon the Broughton household, creating a shadow over the festivities of the Christmas season.  With the memories of Christmas now in the back of our minds, the family's attention was firmly fixed on Nana, whose illness had taken a turn for the worse overnight.

Mam watched with growing concern as her mother's condition deteriorated.  Despite Grandad's insistence, they were unable to reach the family doctor as it was a public holiday.  Mam feared the worst and hurried to the telephone box on Wharf Street to dial 999, desperately seeking help for her very poorly mother.

Nana, weakened by her illness, offered no resistance to the decision to call for an ambulance.  She had battled chest problems for most of her life, and now, as her strength weakened, she knew she needed medical assistance more than ever.  The ambulance crew placed her carefully on the stretcher, ready to be transported to the hospital.  But before she was taken away, she reached out and grasped Mam's hand, her voice barely a whisper amid the chaos.

"I won't be coming back this time, I've had enough!" Nana murmured, her words heavy with resignation.

Mam's heart tightened at her mother's words, understanding the gravity of the situation, but she refused to let despair take hold.  My trembling hand squeezed Nana's frail fingers, offering what comfort I could.  Mam whispered, trying to fill her voice with a courage that I, somehow, knew she didn't feel.

"You'll be back before you know it, Mam.  Stay strong,"

Mam was unaware I had overheard their words. Confusion and fear mingled in my young mind as I turned to Mam, seeking answers.

"Mam, what did Nana mean?", as my voice trembled with uncertainty.  "Is she going to be alright?  I don't want her to die".  Mam gathered me into her arms, her own heart heavy with worry.  With tears threatening to spill, I searched for the right words to soothe Mam's fears, while silently praying for Nana to get better. Together, with the uncertainty of Nana's illness, the Broughton family clung to hope, our love for each other supporting us in our darkest hour.

Uncle Ben arrived at the house.  Fortunately, he had just bought a second-hand car and was able to take Mam and Grandad to the hospital.  Dottie next door offered to look after me whilst they were gone but Mam noticed just how worried I was and decided to let me go with them and hope the hospital would allow me to see Nana.

We arrived at Leicester General Hospital and my heart sank as I learned of the strict policy forbidding children from visiting.  Tears welled in my eyes as I pleaded with Mam to allow me to see Nana, desperate for a glimpse of her amid the uncertainty of what was happening.  Mam hesitated, torn between following the rules and easing my distress.  Sensing my desperation, she relented, albeit with a heavy heart.

"Just for a moment, Anna, go around the back and you should be able to see her", Mam murmured, her voice weak with uncertainty.

I dashed towards the rear of the hospital, my legs ignoring any obstacles in my path.  I ran faster, driven by my one desire to see my beloved Nana.  Breathless but undeterred, I arrived at the balcony where I knew she was going to be, my heart pounding with running.  The railings that protected the balcony windows were quite easy to climb and my fingers clenched them tightly as I leaned forward, my eyes searching eagerly for a glimpse of Nana.

And there she was, Nana, her face bathed in the soft glow of the evening light.  A smile broke across her lips as she spotted me, her eyes glowing with love and warmth.  My heart lifted as I locked eyes with her, my fears momentarily forgotten in the embrace of our shared connection.

We reluctantly left Nana's side and stepped away from the sterile hospital surroundings, unaware that it would be our final farewell.  With a mixture of sadness and determination, I blew another kiss to my beautiful Nana and waved frantically, as if trying to etch my farewell into her very being.  In the years to come, I often reflected on that moment.  The knowledge that I was the last person to see Nana alive filled me with a strange sense of satisfaction, as if it was a poignant and inevitable part of our bond.  Though the pain of loss lingered, there was a bittersweet comfort in knowing that our goodbye was sealed with my final wave.

As soon as we returned home, I rushed upstairs, my tears flowing freely.  The fear of losing Nana consumed my young heart.  Despite my tender age, I possessed a wisdom beyond my years, understanding the severity of the situation.  I sensed that life was about to change in ways I couldn't imagine.

I turned to prayer, seeking relief in my faith.  I remembered the words of my Sunday School teacher, Miss Jane, who had spoken of Jesus' comforting presence during times of distress. With sincere devotion, I knelt beside my bed, pouring out my heart in a plea for Nana's recovery. Each word of my prayer was filled with hope and desperation.

Mam respected my need to grieve and pray. After giving me space to release my emotions, she joined me in the bedroom. We cuddled together, Mam gently soothing my fears while we spoke openly about our worries and hopes for Nana's health. In that moment of vulnerability and faith, Mam's cuddle gave me strength in the belief that our prayers would be heard. And though uncertainty loomed over us, we clung to the love that united us.

The second day of the new year dawned and I awoke unusually early, my mind filled with worry. To my surprise, both Grandad and Mam were already up, their usual weekday routines disrupted by the weight of uncertainty surrounding Nana's health. They gathered around the breakfast table, a gloomy atmosphere surrounding them in silence.

Neither Grandad nor Mam went to work that day. The morning passed quietly, each of them lost in their thoughts, wondering anxiously about Nana's condition. Plans had been made for Ben, Mam's brother, to pick us up from home once he had finished his shift at the Imperial Typewriter Company later that evening.

As the clock approached 6 p.m., Ben's expected arrival time, a sudden knock at the door shattered the stillness of the house.  Mam hurried to answer, her heart pounding with apprehension.  The urgent manner of the knock sent a shiver down her spine, and she knew instinctively that something was terribly wrong.  Fred Wilson, the landlord of the Prince of Wales pub, stood on our doorstep, his expression grave.  Mam's worst fears were confirmed in an instant.  Nana had passed away.

Grandad, Ben, and I gathered in the hallway, all drawn there by Mam's reaction.  Our faces dropped with shock and disbelief as we absorbed the devastating news.  Fred, sympathetically relaying the message, offered his assistance, knowing that the family had no telephone to contact the hospital.

In the aftermath of the devastating news, I was engulfed in a whirlwind of emotions I couldn't fully understand.  Nana's death was crushing and I felt an overwhelming sense of numbness that rendered me stunned and speechless.

My heart ached.  Within the chaos of my thoughts, I had countless questions to ask.  How could I ever find happiness now that Nana had gone?  How could I ease Mam's tears, stemming the flow of grief that threatened to consume us all?  And how could I summon the courage to be strong for my family when my own heart felt so heavy with sorrow?  Alone with my thoughts, I struggled to weather the storm of emotions raging within me.

I felt a desperate need for someone to confide in, someone who could understand the depths of my pain and offer understanding in our grief. I longed to protect Mam from further distress, to spare her the sight of tears that mirrored her own.

# Eighteen

*O*n the Sunday following Nana's death, I felt a deep emptiness clawing at my heart.  Alongside the grief, there was a place of comfort calling my name: Sunday school and the supporting presence of Miss Jane.  I stepped into the chapel, my eyes brimming with tears as Miss Jane sensed the sadness in the air.  Without a word, I rushed into her arms and with tears running down my face, Miss Jane hugged me warmly.  There, in that sacred space, I poured out my sorrow, finding peace in the comforting presence of my friend and teacher.

Miss Jane had known this moment would come.  She had seen the signs of Nana's declining health and had prepared herself to be a source of strength when the time came.  Together, we spoke of memories cherished, of the pain of loss, and the promise of healing.

Joined by my friends in the Sunday school class, I found their shared prayers helped me such a lot.  They lifted their voices in prayer, seeking comfort for me and my family and peace for my departed grandmother's soul.  In that moment of collective faith, I felt a glimmer of hope through the darkness of my grief.

The kindness and support shown by Miss Jane that day left an indelible mark on my heart.  Her words of wisdom, her compassionate embrace, all would be etched into my memory forever.

Miss Jane walked me home once the Sunday school session drew to a close. She was a silent pillar of support by my side. She knew that my journey through grief had only just begun, but with her guidance, I felt a newfound sense of strength and readiness to face the demands that lay ahead.

As Mam managed her own grief, I stepped up to offer my support. I became her constant companion, a source of comfort in our shared sorrow. Yet, beneath my outward strength, I was struggling to come to terms with my own emotions.

The loss of Nana had left me feeling empty, my once bright future now clouded by doubt and fear. The thought of facing the world without her guidance and love seemed daunting, and I started to withdraw from the world around me. I made excuses to avoid social gatherings, preferring the solitude of my own thoughts to the company of others. Swimming, once a favourite pastime, now held little appeal, the weight of my grief making it difficult to find any pleasure in the activities I once loved.

Even at school, my attendance became inconsistent as I grappled with my emotions, my mind often consumed by memories of Nana and fears about the future.  The once bright and outgoing girl now seemed lost in a sea of sadness, my spirits dampened by the enormity of my loss.

Slowly but surely, I began to find pleasure in the love and memories I shared with Nana.  Though the pain of my loss would always linger, I knew her spirit lived on in the love and memories we shared, guiding me through the darkest of days and lighting the path toward a brighter tomorrow.

I found joy in my new companion, Mickey, my beautiful green budgie.  Despite neglecting him since Christmas, I now felt I needed to confide in him, sharing my sorrow.  Remarkably, it seemed as though Mickey understood me, perched quietly, attentively watching me. Wanting to encourage a closer connection with him, I decided to open Mickey's cage, hoping he would venture out.  However, Mickey seemed hesitant.

Mam suggested using a pencil to coax him out.  I persisted until, after numerous attempts, Mickey tentatively perched on the pencil, although he quickly retreated at the slightest movement from me.  I was undeterred.  I continued and Mickey eventually hopped onto the pencil without hesitation.  Thrilled by our progress, I began to train Mickey, guiding him in and out of his cage until he could manage it independently. Gradually, I extended my hand, and Mickey, now acquainted with me and trusting me, hopped onto my fingers.

Suddenly, Mickey became the centre of my world. I was determined to teach him tricks and phrases, wanting him to respond to my every command. With patience and persistence, I trained Mickey to mimic my words, repeating 'Mickey's a pretty boy,' with increasing clarity. Our bond strengthened as he learned to hop onto my fingers and onto the table at my command.

I was intrigued by Mickey's playful nature so I introduced a tiny ball onto the table. To my delight, Mickey eagerly engaged in a game of back-and-forth, pushing the ball with his beak whenever I rolled it towards him. I felt a great companionship in Mickey's presence. It seemed as though he understood my need for love and friendship, responding to my affection and attention. Mickey had become an integral part of my life, bringing light and laughter into my days when I needed it most. Our time together was enjoyable and rewarding.

I had also rediscovered my passion for swimming and was determined to challenge myself by swimming a mile. With dedication and perseverance, I began the daunting task and successfully completed it in an impressive time, a feat that would undoubtedly make Mam immensely proud.

Encouraged by my swimming accomplishment, I also reignited my love for dance.  Despite the time I had missed, I promised myself to make up for it with hard work and determination, setting my sights on achieving my Silver Medal.

Although moments of sadness still lingered, I channelled my efforts towards making Nana proud, and also Mam.  With each triumph, I felt closer to honouring Nana's memory, fuelling my drive to succeed and pushing myself to new heights.

# Nineteen

*M*am used the weekends to introduce me to new experiences, broadening my horizons beyond the confines of our neighbourhood.  One of our favourite destinations was Abbey Park, a quiet retreat just a short walk from our home.  I felt a sense of wonder and tranquillity as I strolled along the park's many pathways. The air was alive with the chatter of birds and the gentle rustle of leaves, creating a serene ambiance that was both comforting and invigorating.  The bridge over the River Soar served as a gateway to our destination, guiding Mam and me towards the heart of Abbey Park.

As we crossed the bridge, the park's pretty pavilion lay ahead of us, surrounded by lush greenery and fragrant blooms.  Its quaint charm and inviting atmosphere beckoned us like a shelter of warmth and comfort.  Mam and I shared stories and laughter over cups of steaming tea and buttery biscuits.

There were many attractions in Abbey Park.  Mam and I often found ourselves drawn to the park's aviary. Walking through the aviary, we experienced the fluttering wings and melodious chirps of the birds and we marvelled at the beautiful array of colours and species on display.

But it was the Abbey ruins that truly captured my imagination. With moss-covered stones and weathered arches, the ruins stood as silent keepers, witnesses of a bygone era lost to human memory. Undeterred by their age and decay, I would climb on top of the low walls, my footsteps echoing through the centuries-old corridors of time. Each of my steps along the well-maintained walls was an adventure in itself, a chance to connect with the rich history and heritage of Abbey Park. I imagined the lives of those who had walked these same paths centuries before. I traced the shapes of the ancient stones, their stories whispering through the rustling leaves. I explored every nook and cranny of the Abbey ruins, uncovering hidden chambers and secret passageways hidden within the ivy-covered walls.

There's something about old stonework, something that calms. In the moments of quiet solitude in the Abbey ruins, I felt a sense of peace and belonging that I had never experienced before. And, as I gazed out over the tranquil expanse of the park, I knew that this was a place I would return to time and time again, a peaceful retreat from the chaos of the world.

The Abbey Park Show was a much-loved tradition that never failed to bring us pleasure. The anticipation leading up to the event was palpable, the excitement building as the August Bank Holiday weekend approached.

A colourful scene greeted us as we stepped into the park grounds on the first day of the show.  Stalls filled with varieties of merchandise lined the pathways, attracting visitors with their array of goods.  The air was filled with the sound of laughter and chatter, and the occasional squeal of delight from children enjoying the fairground rides.

Our first stop was always the family pets' corner, where adorable rabbits and guinea pigs captivated our hearts.  Mam and I couldn't resist spending some time fussing over the fluffy creatures before moving on to explore more of the festivities.

One of the main attractions that never failed to draw our attention was the miniature railway, an annual favourite among visitors of all ages.  We joined the queue, eagerly awaiting our turn to take a ride around the park, relishing the feeling of nostalgia as it chugged along the tracks.

Inside the massive tent housing the flower show, we were greeted by breath-taking sights and the aroma of flowers.  Rows upon rows of meticulously arranged blooms filled the space, their beautiful colours and delicate petals a feast for the eyes.  Mam and I strolled through the displays, marvelling at the skill and artistry on show.

But perhaps the highlight of our day was the horse show.  We found a spot by the ring and settled in to watch as the majestic animals trotted and galloped with grace and poise.  Cheers erupted from the crowd as each rider showcased their skill, and Mam and I found ourselves swept up in the excitement of the moment.

The sun began to set and we made our way towards the bank of the River Soar.  We found a cosy spot to sit and watch as the sky above us came alive with bursts of colour and light.  The grand finale of the Abbey Park show was a glittering firework display that never failed to leave us in awe.

We felt a sense of nostalgia for the park of years past as we gazed out over the tranquil waters of the river.  We reminisced about the park's original features such as the American Garden and the Pavilion, lost to a tragic fire in 1959.  We imagined the elegance of the 19th-century City of Leicester Show, a celebration of the park's horticultural splendour that had once been the pride of the city.

Mam often treated me to a special outing to the Odeon cinema.  Situated in Rutland Street, not far from Wharf Street, the grand theatre became a shelter for us both, offering us an escape into other times, other worlds and, often, romance, all in the magic that was cinema.

An usherette would guide Mam and I to our seats, her torch casting a warm glow in the dimly lit theatre. We settled into our seats, the plush cushions shrouding us in comfort as we shared a tub of popcorn. The aroma of buttery goodness filled the air, adding to the fun of the cinematic experience about to unfold. With the lights dimming and the screen coming to life, our eyes widened with wonder. Surrounded by the magic of the silver screen, Mam and I forged memories that would last a lifetime.

One particular film that left a lasting impression on me was 'Blue Hawaii.' As the vibrant scenes unfolded before me, I was captivated by the story and enthralled by the music. But it was the appearance of my favourite star, Elvis Presley, that truly stole my heart, filling me with excitement.

I often wondered why Mam seemed content to prioritise my happiness over her own social life. I tried to encourage her to spend time with her friends from work but Mam consistently reassured me that she was perfectly content spending her time with me. Despite frequent invitations from her workmates for a night out dancing at the Palais de Dance, Mam always declined, particularly as it was a visit to a dance hall. This continuing dedication from Mam puzzled me. I couldn't quite grasp why she didn't seem interested in mingling with her colleagues or enjoying outings with friends.

With the benefit of hindsight, I can now understand why Mam didn't particularly want to go out with her friends or workmates.  I'm certain she would have liked to have had a relationship with someone special.  She deserved companionship, love and support.  However, the reality she faced was harsh.  Being a single mother in her position, finding a man who was willing to commit seriously was no easy feat.  The stakes were high, and she knew it.

Mam's priority was to protect both herself and me from potential heartbreak.  The last thing she wanted was to invite someone into our lives who might leave us more broken than before.  She understood the potential for pain and disappointment, and she couldn't bear the thought of us going through that.

Furthermore, many of her friends were married.  Unlike them, Mam didn't have the luxury of sharing childcare responsibilities with a partner, especially now that Grandad was showing signs of increasing forgetfulness.  With the added responsibility of caring for him, Mam might have felt overwhelmed and unable to commit to social events or to a new relationship.

Though my curiosity persisted, I remained unaware of the complexities and pressures influencing Mam's decisions.  While her love for me was evident, her reluctance to socialise stemmed from a combination of personal concerns and familial responsibilities.  She chose the certainty of our small, safe world over the potential joy and sorrow of romantic entanglements. In doing so, she showed an incredible strength and selflessness. I now see her sacrifices with a clear understanding that escaped me as a child.

In the final weeks leading up to my 11 Plus examination, I found it increasingly challenging to concentrate on my schoolwork. The looming exam would determine whether I would attend the local High School or the nearest Secondary Modern and this made me very anxious. Determined to excel and make Mam proud of my academic achievements, I poured my heart and soul into my studies. As the day of the exam dawned, my stomach churned with a mix of nerves and excitement. The stakes were high, and I knew the importance of performing well to secure a place at the reputable High School. I had worked hard, studying well into the night in preparation for this moment.

When the results were finally unveiled, my heart sank. I had missed out on a place at the High School by just two marks. The disappointment hit me hard, and I couldn't shake off the feeling of failure. In my eyes, I had let Mam down, she had invested so much hope and support in fulfilling my dreams. The sense of defeat lingered like a shadow. It seemed as though all my efforts had been in vain. However, Mam's support, comforting words and reminders of my hard work proved to be a ray of light in my darkest hour.  Mam reminded me that this setback was not the end of the road.

"There will be another opportunity," her voice consoling my wounded pride.  "You can retake the exam when you're thirteen.  This is just a bump in the road, not the end of your journey."  I vowed to grab the next opportunity with both hands, knowing that Mam would be there with every step along the way.

# Twenty

*I*n the heart of the house once inhabited by Nana, a new chapter unfolded.  Mam decided to breathe life into the front room that had long been the room that Nana had occupied.  With a warm smile, she invited me to claim the space.

Mam had hoped that I would be tinkling the ivories of the piano once more.  Despite my lack of formal training in reading sheet music, my knack for picking out popular tunes and translating the melodies into recognisable pieces was undeniable.  My natural understanding of music resonated through every tune I taught myself to play.

Mam revitalised and decorated the room with care.  A cosy two-seater settee invited guests to relax, while delicate ornaments graced the mantelpiece, adding a touch of luxury to the space.  Positioned at the heart of it all, a fashionable coffee table, around which moments of shared laughter and heartfelt conversations took place.

In the quiet confines of the front room, I found calm within the chaos of everyday life.  With each tune I created on the piano, the world outside faded into obscurity, replaced by the endearing sound of melodies and harmonies.  Time seemed to stand still here as I surrendered myself to the appeal of music.  Lost in the rhythm of my own creations, I revelled in the freedom to express myself without restraint.

My eyes widened with excitement on my 11th birthday as I unwrapped one of my gifts: a Dansette record player, resplendent in its red and white glory.  In the exhilarating musical landscape of 1958, such a gift was not just a device for listening to music.  Dansette record players were the epitome of 'cool' in the eyes of young people like me during the height of rock 'n' roll.  With their sleek looks and compact size, they gave off an air of sophistication while also reflecting the dynamic energy of the music they played.  They led a cultural revolution from the front.  But what truly set Dansette players apart was their innovative design.  With the ability to stack several singles at once, I could enjoy hours of uninterrupted music, whether dancing the night away or simply lounging around on lazy weekends.

I placed my favourite vinyl records on the turntable and pressed play. The room filled with the infectious beats of rock 'n' roll and the built-in speakers brought the music to life, filling the air.

In the years to come, my record player would serve as the setting for countless memories: late-night dances, heart-to-heart conversations, and everything in between. It was more than just a piece of technology.  It was a symbol of youth, rebellion, and the transformative power of music.

My love for music extended beyond just playing the piano.  It was deeply rooted in my appreciation of artists who spoke to my soul.  Among them, Elvis Presley held a special place in my heart.  His charisma, his voice, his presence!  Everything about him resonated with me in a profound way.

One day, Mam surprised me with a gift: Elvis Presley's iconic record, 'Jailhouse Rock.'  Overjoyed, I placed the vinyl on the turntable, my fingers trembling with excitement as I lowered the needle onto the groove.  As the opening chords vibrated through the room, I felt a surge of elation and from that moment on, 'Jailhouse Rock' became a precious gem in my collection.  I played it incessantly, each spin of the record breathing new life into the timeless melody.  The compelling rhythm, the raw energy, the defiant spirit captivated me every time, leaving me thirsty for more.

I never grew tired of the record and each spin revealed new modulations, new layers of meaning waiting to be discovered.  It was more than just music to me; it was a journey, an escape into a world where anything was possible.  In the sanctity of the front room, surrounded by the warmth of Mam's love and the pulsating beats of Elvis Presley's music, I found a sense of belonging.  With 'Jailhouse Rock' as my anthem, I danced to the rhythm of my own heart, embracing the magic of music with a deep passion.

Mam was also a lover of music and would often be heard hitting the top notes of a song being played on the radio.  In the heart of our family, music was more than just background noise.  While we each had our own musical preferences, Mam´s appreciation for Vera Lynn was unprecedented.  Though the wartime melodies weren´t exactly at the top of my playlist, Mam´s affection for them was infectious.  Her eyes would light up whenever Vera Lynn´s voice filled the room, as if transported back to a time when those songs held a special meaning.

But music, with its power to arouse both joy and sorrow, wasn´t always a welcome.  There were moments when Mam would silence the radio abruptly, a signal that a song either didn´t resonate with her or stirred up too many painful memories.

The years danced by and Mam remained firm in her love of music, her taste evolving with the changing trends.  While her heart found pleasure in the husky voice and smoochy tunes of Neil Diamond, it was the captivating music of Mario Lanza that truly delighted her soul.

Lanza, with his handsome charm and a voice like velvet, became something very special to Mam. Whether it was his passionate interpretation of 'Be My Love' or the beautiful 'O Sole Mio', each note seemed to resonate deep within her.

Observing Mam's attraction to Lanza's voice, there lingered a question I used to ask myself. Did Mam love the man himself more than his singing? It was a mystery that even to this day remains unanswered. Perhaps it was the combination of both, the music and the man, that brought her such immense pleasure.

There was a beautiful balance in Mam's taste in music, a reflection of her spirit that seemed to resonate with my own. Our shared appreciation for artists like Neil Diamond and the variety of melodies of the James Last Orchestra wasn't merely a coincidence.

Mam's love for music was obvious, especially during those cherished family occasions that brought us all together. She was unable to sit down once the lights dimmed, the disco played and the glitter ball displayed colourful lights around the room. Uncle Ben, who was also a good dancer, would grab her hand and they took over the dance floor, determined to have a good time.

When I was making one of my regular visits to see Mam years later, I could hear the sounds of music and laughter coming from the inside of her living room. Peering through the window, I was met with a heart-warming sight. Mam, a twinkle in her eye, was dancing around the room with her granddaughter, Gemma, held tightly in her arms.

The catching melody of 'Search for a Hero' by M People, including Heather Small, filled the room as they swayed with easy movements, lost in the music.  Their laughter rang out, merging with the lyrics as they sang at the top of their voices,

"You've got to search for the hero inside yourself," enjoying every minute of one of Mam's favourite songs.

I remained outside, content simply to watch, not wanting to intrude upon their precious time together.  It was a simply magical moment, profoundly meaningful. A grandmother and her granddaughter sharing a love of music and of each other.

During Mam's later years, there were two artists who held a special place in her heart: Abba and Celine Dion. Their music, with its timeless appeal and poignant lyrics, became more than just a source of entertainment.  They were Mam's lifeline, her source of comfort and feelings of love during her battles with illness.  In the midst of pain and uncertainty, the songs of Abba and Celine Dion became symbols of hope, casting light into the darkest corners of her life.  Their melodies wrapped her in a cocoon of calm, offering an intense peace that surpassed the boundaries of sickness and suffering.

And so, as we journeyed through life's highs and lows, it was the music of these artists that became our constant companion, weaving its way through our memories and binding us together in a symphony of love.

Even now, 25 years after Mam's death, the music of Abba and Celine Dion still feature very much in our lives.

Auntie June with Colin. Nana
and me 1950

Great Grandad James Broughton and
Grandad Albert Broughton 1958

My nursery days. I am fifth from left. 1948

Mam with her brothers
Edward and Ben. 1932

Land Army Days.
Mam is standing 4th
from left next to
bridegroom. 1944

Colin on the step
and me with my pram
1949

Me and Carol.1953
Queen Elizabeth II
Coronation.

Miss Jane 2nd right, back row. Carley St. Chapel 1958

Lido de Jesolo
1965

Mam with Dutch
lady 1963

Mary and Edward
John and Glenis
1965

Mam and Ben 1993

and me

Mam

Nana

Our legacy,
Mam's
Grandchildren

Paul    Gemma    Dave

# Twenty-One

*T*he disappointment of my 11 Plus results gradually eased and I began to look forward to a future in a new school. The summer of 1958 approached and I bid farewell to Taylor Street School, where I had spent my unforgettable infant, primary and junior school days. I had fond memories of Taylor Street but was also excited by the prospect of starting anew at Dale Girls Secondary Modern on Melbourne Road.

The transition marked a significant change for me. Taylor Street had been local and near to home. Dale Girls, on the other hand, was located further away on Melbourne Road, necessitating a much longer walk. However, logistical considerations dictated the choice of school, and I found myself offered a place at Dale Girls.

Though I looked forward to the new adventure with enthusiasm, I couldn't shake a hint of apprehension. The unfamiliarity of a new school and the prospect of making new friends were my worries. There was comfort in knowing that two other girls from my junior class would also be attending Dale Girls, offering a small taste of familiarity amid the sea of new faces.

In the weeks leading up to the start of term, Mam busied herself with the task of purchasing my school uniform. Each item held significance, symbolising my journey into adolescence and the changes that lay ahead. First came the navy gym slip, a type of pinafore dress, a symbol of my newfound status as a senior school student, paired with a crisp white blouse, a tie with navy and yellow stripes, and the addition of navy knickers to wear during PE or other sporting events. The blazer, decorated with the school emblem, held a special place in Mam's heart. As we carefully selected the garment, I couldn't help but feel a swell of pride. It was a real indication of my academic status and the bright future that lay ahead of me.

As I tried on each piece of my uniform, I couldn't deny the bittersweet emotions I was feeling. The comfort of childhood was giving way to the excitement and the uncertainty of adolescence. With each button fastened and each seam adjusted, my outward appearance mirrored the internal transformation taking place.

The years had flown by, and I stood on the edge of adulthood, ready to embrace the opportunities and challenges that lay ahead. I donned my newly acquired uniform, feeling empowered and proud. I was ready to embark on this new chapter of my life, armed with the love and support of Mam.

I enjoyed the sense of liberation that came with attending an all-girls school. I had endured the hurtful taunts and jeers from boys at my junior school, who cruelly labelled me as 'fatty.' Each insult chipped away at my self-esteem, leaving me feeling insecure and unworthy. Now, surrounded by my female peers at my new school, I found refuge from the relentless scrutiny of boys. Without the constant barrage of hurtful remarks, I felt a weight lift from my shoulders. No longer did I have to endure the piercing stares or the mocking laughter that had plagued me at my previous school. In this all-girls environment, I discovered a sense of confidence and self-assurance. Freed from the burden of judgment, I blossomed into my own skin, embracing my individuality with pride. No longer defined by the cruel words of others, I flourished in an atmosphere of acceptance and support, my smile growing brighter, my laughter more carefree.

I loved the sociability of my classmates, cherishing the friendships that bloomed in this nurturing environment. Here, I was celebrated for who I was, free of the shallow expectations imposed by others.

However, I didn't enjoy the way I and the other pupils in Year 1 were treated as the 'babies' of the school. Despite the relief of escaping the taunts from boys, I was now facing a new challenge within the hierarchy of the school.

In the eyes of the older students, Year 1 pupils were deemed inexperienced newcomers, still finding their footing in the vast landscape of secondary education.

We were often subject to patronising attitudes and dismissed as immature.  It angered me to be labelled a 'baby' simply because I was in Year 1.  I longed to be seen as capable and independent, not coddled or underestimated.  The arrogance grated on my nerves, igniting a desire to prove myself and break free from the confines of the 'infant' label.

Despite my frustrations, I refused to let myself be defined by the perceptions of others.  With determination and my chin up, I set out to prove that being in Year 1 didn't equate to weakness or incompetence.  I worked hard to excel academically and assert myself in extracurricular activities, determined to show that I was just as capable as any other student in the school.  I eventually began to earn the respect of my peers and teachers alike.  My perseverance and determination shone through, dispelling any notion of my being a mere 'baby' in the school hierarchy.

Regardless of my previous aversion to sports, I discovered a newfound enthusiasm for hockey and netball.  It wasn't long before I realised that I had a natural talent for both.  My skills on the field were undeniable, and I quickly became an essential part of my team's success.  The sense of accomplishment that came from excelling in these sports was exhilarating, boosting my confidence and self-esteem.

But perhaps even more importantly, I found a sense of belonging within my team.  In the heat of competition, I felt unity and purpose, bonded by a shared goal and a mutual respect for each other's abilities.  As I darted across the hockey field or passed the ball with precision on the netball court, I felt liberated.  Here, I was valued not for my appearance or popularity, but for my skills and dedication to my team.  With each game won and every goal scored, my passion for hockey and netball grew stronger and stronger.

Within my first year of senior school, I was excelling in practical subjects such as needlework and cookery, while struggling with academic ones, although music, geography and religious instruction were subjects I also enjoyed.  Despite my best efforts, I was disheartened to be consistently near the lower end of test results.  The disappointment tormented me, sapping my motivation and leading to a lack of concentration in class.

I desperately wanted to succeed in all my subjects, but my repeated setbacks pulled me down.  Frustrated and demoralised, it became increasingly difficult to focus, often becoming restless and disruptive in class.  My behaviour drew reprimands from my teachers, further adding to my sense of failure.

Deep down, I knew that Mam would be disappointed in my behaviour.  The thought of letting down the one person who had always believed in me was hard to bear.

Despite my best intentions, I was unable to break free from the cycle of disappointment and distraction.

I yearned for the sense of accomplishment that had eluded me so far, but the path to success seemed increasingly elusive.  The weight of expectation, both from myself and from others, bore down on my shoulders, threatening to crush my spirit.  In the midst of my struggles, I clung to the hope that I could turn things around.  I knew that I had the potential to succeed; I just needed to find a way to unlock it.

There was another sadness in my path: my bicycle, faithful companion though it was, was now too small for me.  The question was, how could I replace it?

Walking home from school one afternoon, the only thing on my mind was finding a way to earn some money.  I decided to stop by Green's newsagents on Humberstone Road to enquire about paper rounds.  I hadn't discussed this with Mam, as I wanted to gather more information first.  Mr. Green, the manager, greeted me warmly.  I expressed my interest in paper rounds, and he informed me that there was one evening round available.  The job entailed delivering 60 Leicester Mercury newspapers, 6 days a week, to houses around the area.  He offered me 2/6s a week (12½p).

I listened attentively, already calculating how this could help me save up for a new bike and other things I wanted.  However, I knew I needed Mam's approval before committing to anything.  Politely, I told Mr. Green that I would need to discuss it with Mam and promised to return after school the next day for a final decision.  With that, I left the newsagents, my mind racing with possibilities for the future.

I stood outside Mam´s factory, situated at the lower end of Crafton Street, waiting patiently for her to clock out of her shift.  When she saw me, she was surprised and curious as to why I was there.  I wasted no time in explaining about the paper round opportunity at Green's and asked if I could take it on.  Mam, though a bit apprehensive at first, knew Mr. Green's shop as she often stopped by for her daily packet of 5 Senior Service cigarettes, and a copy of 'Judy', my weekly comic.

"Why do you want to do a paper round?", Mam asked, wanting to understand my motivations.  My eyes sparkled with enthusiasm as I replied,

"Because I want to buy myself a new bike!"  Mam couldn't help but smile at my determination.  She knew how much I longed for a new bike and admired my initiative in seeking out a way to earn the money for it. With a nod, Mam gave her permission, feeling proud of my drive and independence.

The next afternoon, I made my way back to Green's newsagents to confirm my decision with Mr. Green.

With a determined expression, I informed him that I was ready to take on the paper round. Mr. Green looked at me seriously, emphasising the importance of reliability.

"You must promise not to let me down," he said sternly. He explained that if I ever found myself unable to complete the round due to illness or other reasons, I should try to find a friend to cover for me. However, I would be expected to pay my friend for their service.

"Be here on Monday at 5pm sharp," Mr. Green instructed firmly, ensuring I understood the commitment I was making. I nodded eagerly, assuring Mr. Green that I would fulfil my responsibilities without fail. I left the newsagents, determination burning within me, ready to start my new adventure as a paper girl.

I couldn't contain my excitement as I begged Mam to visit Maurice Birch's shop on Saturday to check out the bicycles he had in stock. Mam understood my eagerness but also knew the financial implications. Buying a bicycle would likely mean going through hire purchase. Mam had been a loyal customer of Birch's for years, purchasing everything from light bulbs to a new electric boiler for our kitchen. She knew that Maurice always provided good quality products and reasonable payment plans and trusted him to offer a fair deal.

Despite the financial considerations, Mam couldn't resist my enthusiasm. As we entered Maurice Birch's shop on that Saturday, my eyes immediately fixed onto a beautiful blue bicycle made by Raleigh.  It was love at first sight; I was enamoured by the bike's sleek design and reputable make.

Mam couldn't help but notice the price tag attached to the bicycle; £18/2s/6d was a considerable sum. However, Mam also acknowledged that it could be paid for at a manageable rate of 5/- a month (equivalent to 25p) over 3years.  Despite my excitement, Mam displayed concerns about committing to such a purchase, especially considering the uncertainty of my commitment to my new paper round.  I eagerly reassured her.  I promised to dedicate myself to the paper round and prove my reliability.  Yet Mam remained cautious, insisting that I must try the paper round first before making any commitments.  She proposed that I give her the entire 10/- of my first month's wages as a demonstration of my commitment and responsibility.

Though disappointed by the delay, I understood Mam's reasoning and agreed to the terms.  With determination in my heart and dreams of riding my new blue Raleigh bicycle, I prepared myself for the challenge of my upcoming paper round, eager to prove myself worthy of Mam's trust and the coveted bike.  As promised, I diligently completed my paper round for a full month, earning my first month's wages of 10/-.  True to my word, I handed the money to Mam, proud of my accomplishment.

The following Saturday, Mam and I made our way to Maurice Birch's shop once again. It was very exciting to approach the store front where my dream bicycle was waiting for me. Maurice greeted us warmly, recognising us from our previous visit. With a smile, I pointed to the blue Raleigh bicycle I had fallen in love with a month earlier. Mam, seeing the sparkle in my eyes, nodded in agreement.

We completed the purchase without hesitation, securing the beloved bicycle that rewarded my hard work. We wheeled the bicycle out of the shop, my heart swelled with excitement. I couldn't wait to ride it. Together, we walked home, made happy by the fulfilment of my dream.

I was the tender age of 11½ when I embarked on my first venture into the world of responsibility with my paper round. Each evening after school, I would mount my bicycle and pedal through the quiet streets of my neighbourhood. My large sack filled with newspapers was slung over my shoulder, a tangible reminder of the task at hand. Despite the encroaching darkness and the weight of my load, I found satisfaction in the rhythmic whirl of my bicycle wheels against the pavement. My mind buzzed with energy, driven by the melodies that danced through my thoughts. Music was my constant companion, a soundtrack to my daily routine that uplifted my spirit and encouraged my determination. As I travelled the usual streets, my favourite tunes would sound in my head to the beat of the pedals.

With each paper delivered I was not just a girl on a bicycle; I was a guardian of information, delivering the news to my neighbours with diligence and care. Despite the challenges and uncertainties that lay ahead, I pedalled on, my spirit enhanced by the music in my heart and the sense of purpose that accompanied me on my nightly journey.

# Twenty-Two

*M*am had set off on her usual Saturday morning visit to Leicester Market for her weekly fruit and vegetables, leaving me at home.  I had decided to stay back to catch up on the homework that I hadn't managed to finish the night before.  One of the reasons for the delay was my indulgence in playtime with my adorable budgie, Mickey.

As I busied myself with my schoolwork, I suddenly remembered something.  My school satchel!  I rushed upstairs to find it but paused when I noticed Mam's bedroom door was open.  My curiosity now triggered, I couldn't resist taking a glance inside.  I was surprised to see that Mam had left the key in her wardrobe; a rare occurrence as I recalled she always kept it locked.

With grandad comfortably settled in front of the crackling fire downstairs and Mam not expected back for some time, my uncontrollable nosiness kicked in.  I saw this as an opportunity to satisfy my inquisitive mind and sneak a peek inside the wardrobe, curious about what secrets it might hold.  With cautious steps, I approached the wardrobe, my heart pounding with excitement and with the enormity of doing what I knew I shouldn't be doing, unaware of the surprises that awaited me inside.

Without much searching, I stumbled upon a black bag tucked away at the back of the wardrobe, a bag I had never seen before. It was securely closed with a clasp that sprung open with a gentle press. Intrigued, I peered inside and found it filled with an assortment of odds and ends and purses.

One thing immediately caught my attention: a slightly crumpled envelope that had already been opened. Without hesitation, I reached for the envelope and carefully removed the letter inside and the two photographs that accompanied it.

At first, I slowly opened the envelope, but the possibility of Mam's return made me rush through the letter's content. However, as I glanced over the first few lines, something made me pause. Something in the way the words were written, the tenderness in the address 'My dearest Ellen,' made me slow down and truly absorb the message. The letter, dated July 1947, held a significance I couldn't ignore.

As I continued to read, my eyes widened with surprise. The letter wasn't just a casual correspondence; it was a piece of my own history unfolding before me. The man who wrote it, my father, asked if he could name their new baby daughter 'Anna Elizabeth'. He was giving me my name! My heart skipped a beat at the realisation of the intimate connection I shared with the sender of this letter.

But the surprises didn't end there.  My eyes darted to the bottom of the page, where I discovered my father's name: Matthew.  And then, scanning back to the top, I learned he lived in Folkestone, Kent.

With each word, the letter peeled back layers of mystery surrounding my father's absence from my life.  His explanation for leaving Mam alone and broken was both heart-breaking and illuminating.  He promised to return, to marry Mam once he had resolved his marital situation.  My heart sank, I realised that promise would never be fulfilled.

With this new knowledge invading my mind, I couldn't help but feel a mix of emotions.  There was sadness for the broken family I never knew and a fierce determination to uncover the truth about my father and the life he left behind.

My twelfth birthday was approaching.  With a clarity far beyond my age, I pieced together the fragments of my family's story.  The letter illuminated the shadows that had long cloaked my understanding of my own origins.  It explained why Mam had always avoided answering questions about my absent father, why I alone among my friends didn't have a daddy to call my own, and why the laughter of siblings was absent from our home.  But more importantly, it gave me an understanding of why Mam used to cry into her pillow at night.

With quiet understanding, I carefully replaced the letter and photographs into the envelope, ensuring that every item was arranged exactly as I had found them.  I closed the wardrobe door and turned the key, taking care to leave the room undisturbed, and exactly as it was.

Leaving Mam's bedroom, I felt the weight of my secret bearing down on me.  I knew that the knowledge I had uncovered must remain hidden, tucked away from prying eyes and probing questions.  The risk of revealing my secret exploration was too great, and I couldn't bear the thought of Mam finding out about my snooping, about breaking her trust at the first opportunity.

Over the years, I carried the memory of that day with me, the letter and the photographs and their revelations firmly etched into my mind.  Though I dared not speak of it, the information I had discovered would serve as a guiding light in my quest to uncover the truth about my father.

After Mam's death in 1999, I was grappling between a profound sense of loss and unfinished business. Mam's absence left a huge void, but it also opened a door to something I had long suppressed: the need to uncover the truth about my father.  It was a quest I had never wished to begin while Mam was alive, fearful of the betrayal and pain it might inflict upon her.  But now that she was gone, I felt an undeniable urge for closure, a need to put the missing piece of my life's puzzle into place.

Determined, I began my search.  I delved into old photographs, letters, and any fragment of information that might lead me to the man who had been absent from my life for so long.  As I uncovered clues and pieced together fragments of my father's story, I couldn't help but wonder about the man behind the mystery.  What had led him to leave Mam and me behind?  Did he ever think of us?  Did he regret his choices?

I could still visualise the photographs I had found in Mam's handbag all those years ago, images of Matthew as a milkman and as a musician in a brass band and I carried them with me in my mind as I delved deeper into my family's history.

Finally, the pieces began to fall into place.  During a two-day visit to Folkestone and its library in 2004, my friend, Felicity and I scoured the library records, newspapers, directories, parish records, anything we could get our hands on.  We were determined to uncover the mysteries of my father's family history, spanning over a century.  We managed to trace 100 years of connections, information and stories, but a key question remained unanswered: was Matthew dead or alive?

As Saturday lunchtime approached, the library announced its closure.  Felicity and I had planned to drive home, but the thought of leaving without a definitive answer was heart-breaking.  We sat on a bench outside the library, staring at the red telephone box that stood nearby.  Felicity, ever resourceful, suggested we check the telephone directory as a last resort.  And then, like a light in the darkness, she found a name: Caroline, Matthew's sister, living in Folkestone.  We sat there, stunned, the directory clutched in her hands.  This was real.  I had a tangible lead, one that could finally complete the jigsaw puzzle I had been trying to piece together for years.

At that moment, I was shaking and crying, not knowing what I was about to find out.  The library doors were closed, but a new door had just opened.  I knew we had to make a decision.  Should we ring her, or go home?  We rang.

Felicity contacted Caroline and explained who I was, revealing that her brother, Matthew, could possibly be my father.  After a moment of stunned silence, Caroline confirmed that my father was, indeed, alive.  Shocked and surprised, she agreed to meet us.  Later that day, we found ourselves in the quiet surroundings of Caroline's home.  My 91-year-old aunt welcomed us warmly, her eyes reflecting years of wisdom and untold stories.  As we stepped inside, my breath caught in my throat.  Enlarged, framed, and hanging proudly on the walls were the very same photographs I had discovered in

Mam's handbag all those years ago.  Both in black and white and enlarged, one was of Matthew in his milkman's apron standing next to his milk cart and the other was of him playing the trombone with his brass band.

Seeing these photos again was the moment of confirmation.  Each proved beyond any doubt that Matthew was, indeed, my father and that I had found his family.

At the age of 54, I had found the missing piece of my puzzle.

# Twenty-three

*T*he winter of 1959 settled in and my connection to Carley Street Chapel remained solid, providing me with a place of warmth and of community.  My faith had become a foundation of my life, guiding me through the ups and downs with ongoing strength.

I had outgrown Sunday school, finding it too juvenile for my maturing understanding.  However, I remained dedicated to my spiritual journey so, I began attending services later on Sunday evenings and on Thursdays, not only eager to deepen my connection to my faith but to meet up with people and create more friendships along the way.

One desire burned within my heart; to be baptised within the walls of the chapel I held so dear.  It was a longing I talked about with Miss Jane, the wonderful lady who had become a mentor and a friend.  With Miss Jane's support, arrangements were made for my baptism.

I had seen the baptismal ceremony performed many times before.  However, the anticipation built as the date approached until, finally, on the 11th of May 1960, I stood before the chapel's congregation, excited and admiring the sight in front of me.  They had removed part of the floor to reveal a large pool, shimmering in the soft glow of candlelight.  I stepped into the water, surrounded by the loving support of Mam and my church family and felt profound peace within me. The moment I was baptised, I felt as though a weight had been lifted from my shoulders, replaced by deep belonging and acceptance.

I emerged from the water, emotional with joy and gratitude. I knew that this was a moment I would carry with me for the rest of my life. From that day forward, my journey took on a new depth and meaning.

My passion for dance continued to blossom and I found myself drawn to new experiences that would further drive my love for movement and music. One such place that was close to my heart was the Palais de Dance situated in Humberstone Gate, a renowned dance hall that had become a beloved hotspot for the residents of Leicester.

On Saturday mornings, some of my school friends and I would make our way to the Palais, eager to immerse ourselves in the vibrant atmosphere and rhythmic beats that filled the air. It was the one out-of-school activity I wholeheartedly embraced, a place where I could lose myself in the world of dance.

We stepped into the grand hall to be greeted by the sight of the glittering disco ball casting shimmering circles of light across the dance floor, illuminating the dancers below in a dazzling display. The music flowed through my veins, urging me to join the crowd of dancers moving to the rhythm, their dresses gleaming in the soft light. The seating booths that lined the sides of the hall stood out with their luxurious red velvet seats, a touch of elegance that I had rarely encountered before. It was a sight that I admired, a glimpse into a world of glamour and sophistication.

I returned to the Palais for many years, each visit leaving me with a treasure trove of happy memories and new friendships found on the dance floor. However, it was the music and the sheer exhilaration of dance, above all else, that kept me going back time and time again.

As winter approached and the nights grew longer, I was content to enjoy the simple pleasures of my spare evenings, filling my time with activities that I loved. On some evenings, I would head to the swimming baths, relishing the sensation of the cool water against my skin as I glided through the lanes with effortless grace. It was a time for me to unwind and rejuvenate, leaving the stresses of the day behind as I immersed myself in the soothing rhythm of my strokes.

Other evenings were reserved for music, as I retreated to the front room, my favourite records spinning on the turntable. I would lose myself in each well-known tune, letting the rhythms transport me to another world.

But perhaps the most interesting evenings were those spent with Mam as we sat together planning for the future.  We would discuss dreams and ideas over a cup of tea and a biscuit, weaving grand visions of what lay ahead.

On a Sunday, I would often set out on my trusty bicycle, pedalling my way through the quiet country lanes, the crisp air biting at my cheeks as I ventured into the unknown.  I would promise Mam that I would be home before dark to avoid her worrying all day: very rarely did I let her down.

My favourite destination was the town of Loughborough, a bustling hub located eleven miles from Leicester.  I would launch into a circular tour along country routes that took me through the picturesque villages tucked between the gentle hills around Charnwood Forest and Bradgate Park.

With each mile I covered, I felt exhilaration and freedom, the wind whipping through my hair as I sang my favourite tune of the week.  The countryside stretched out before me, a scene of rolling hills and lush greenery that seemed to go on forever.

To support my hobbies and contribute to my family, I took on two paper rounds, one in the morning and another in the evening.  The extra income doubled my spending power, allowing me to indulge in my favourite

pastime: collecting records.  Picking up a copy of the
New Musical Express was a weekly highlight and I
would carefully select the latest chart-toppers to add to
my growing collection.

Like many other magazines, the NME has been a
vital lifeline to the ever-changing music scene.  By
pouring over its pages from front to back, I could stay up
to date with the latest trends and developments,
discovering new genres, new artists and songs that
captured my imagination and fed my passion for music.

Mam and I held a special ritual on Saturday
mornings that we treasured above all else:  a visit to
Cox's Cake Shop.  Near to the corner of our busy street,
the shop presented an irresistible appeal that drew us in
week after week.

Stepping through the door, the tempting aroma of
fresh baking greeted us, calling us closer to the display
cabinet filled with tasty treats.  Half a dozen crusty cobs
and some fresh cream doughnuts were always on our
order, a weekly indulgence that Mam and I, and even
Grandad, eagerly looked forward to.

But we kept returning for more than the delectable
pastries.  We also loved the warm atmosphere and the
friendly faces that greeted us each time we entered.
Tommy Cox, the owner of the shop, could always be
found behind the counter with a twinkle in his eye and a

smile on his face, ready to serve up a dose of cheer along with our morning treats.

If the bakers at the back of the shop were still at work, I would often make my way through the back entrance, curious to see the magic happening behind the scenes.  Tommy's sister, Joan, would be hard at work, kneading dough, shaping pastries, and filling the air with the inviting wafts of freshly baked bread.

Together with the flour-covered counters and the laughter-filled conversations, I discovered I enjoyed the hum of activity.  I felt at home in a way I never had before.  After our freshly baked treats, we would often stay a little longer, soaking in the sights and sounds of the cake shop.  It was a place to satisfy our sweet tooth and enjoy the pleasure of Saturday mornings.

My friendship with the Cox family had blossomed into something truly special, leading to an unexpected opportunity that would change my life in ways I never imagined.  One Saturday morning, as I savoured my usual treats at the cake shop, I was approached by Tommy Cox with an offer that took me by surprise.

"Anna, how would you like to join us on Saturday mornings?" Tommy asked with a warm smile.  My eyes widened in disbelief.  The thought of working alongside my friends at Cox's was thrilling.  I knew it was an opportunity I couldn't refuse.

"Are you serious?" I exclaimed, excited.  Tommy nodded, his smile growing wider.

"Absolutely.  We could use an extra pair of hands, and we know you've got a good head on your shoulders."

I accepted the offer without hesitation, eager to start this new adventure.  From that day forward, I became a vital part of the Cox family business, immersing myself in the world of baking and customer service with limitless enthusiasm.  I thrived on the responsibility that came with my new role, relishing the chance to contribute to the success of the cake shop.  I grew more confident and capable with every passing week, earning the trust and admiration of my colleagues and customers alike.

But perhaps the greatest reward of all was fulfilment and pride that came with earning my own money.  This extra income provided me with the funds to finance my passion for dancing and music with ease, allowing me to pursue my dreams without limitations and not burdening Mam with the responsibility.

As I worked alongside the Cox family, I realised that I had found more than just a job; I had found a second family.  I continued to thrive in my role at the cake shop and knew that I was exactly where I was meant to be, surrounded by friends, pursuing my passions, and embracing every opportunity that came my way.

# Twenty-four

*A*pproaching my teenage years, my school life became a source of both challenge and concern.  Despite my growing confidence and willingness to take on new challenges, my academic struggles remained an ongoing problem.  Mam recognised my reluctance towards attending school and insisted that I always applied my best effort and behaved myself.

The time came for me to sit my 13 plus exam which would determine my eligibility for Moat Girls School, a reputable Grammar School nearby.  Both Mam and I had mixed feelings.  My lack of confidence in academic subjects made it difficult for me to feel adequately prepared for the exam, despite my best efforts to revise.

Mam understood my struggles and appreciated that a move to a different school might not be the best solution for me.  She observed my occasional difficulties and understood that my confidence could suffer with each setback.  While Mam wanted success for me, she prioritised my happiness above all else.  All she asked of me was to do my best, that was all that mattered.

On the day of the exam, I approached the challenge with determination.  Despite my efforts, the exam proved to be an alarming obstacle, concentrating more on the academic subjects in which I lacked competency.  When the results came in, my heart sank as I learned that I had once again fallen short of success.

Although disappointed, Mam reassured me that my worth extended far beyond the confines of a single exam. She reminded me of the many talents and qualities that made me special, knowing that success comes in many forms and that my journey was far from over.

One afternoon during the school holidays, I walked into town alone, my footsteps drawn by the lively atmosphere of the daily market. The air buzzed with the calls of the stall holders, trading their wares as the day wound towards its close. Their voices rose and fell with the urgency of attracting the dwindling shoppers, creating a symphony of commerce that I found oddly comforting.

I strolled into a record store, eager to lose myself in the latest popular tunes from the top twenty list. The rows of headphones beckoned, offering a temporary escape into the world of melody. However, my aimless browsing soon caught the attention of the vigilant shop assistant who politely nudged me towards the exit. Though my time there was brief, it felt well spent, immersed in the rhythms of the music.

One of my favourite shops was Lewis's, where the elegance of its wooden escalators never failed to captivate me. Despite its reputation for higher prices, Mam's expression echoed in my mind: quality comes at a cost, you get what you pay for!

Heading towards the exit onto Humberstone Gate, the enticing displays of the impending school year greeted me from the store fronts.  Among them, a pencil and crayon set caught my eye, its zipped case covered with a lovely bird design.  Overcome by a sudden desire for something new and beautiful, I sneakily slipped it into my bag and made my exit.

But as I stepped through the doorway, a hand on my shoulder shattered my dream.  Panic consumed me as I faced the stern gaze of a security guard, his badge gleaming in the afternoon light.  My heart pounded as he spoke of involving the police, sending waves of fear crashing over me.  Tears streamed down my face as I begged him to let me go and promised that I would never do it again.  He was then joined by a lady store detective who explained that they didn't have to involve the police but only if I came back to the store in the morning with my mother!  My world was turned upside down.  How was I going to tell her?  The prospect of facing Mam's disappointment loomed large as I contemplated the consequence of my actions.

That evening, I reluctantly confessed to my shoplifting, bracing myself for Mam's reaction.  As she listened to my account, her disappointment was evident.

Her tears and subsequent withdrawal hurt deeply, leaving me feeling utterly alone and sorrowful.

The following morning dawned with a sense of dread as Mam and I made our way to Lewis's. The journey felt never ending, each step laden with the weight of impending doom.  Upon arrival, Mam was ushered into a room to discuss the events of the previous day.

Left alone with my thoughts, fear gnawed at me, threatening to consume me entirely.  But, when Mam emerged, her reassuring touch offered comfort through the storm.  The relief was indescribable and I was so thankful that I was not going to be taken to the police station.  This was an event I would never forget and one I would never repeat.

Entering my penultimate year of senior school in 1960, I was drawn into the circle of a group of girls whose behaviour left much to be desired.  They were known for their cheekiness, cockiness, and a tendency to push boundaries in ways that were unacceptable to many. Despite my better judgment, I gravitated towards this group, perhaps enticed by the thrill of rebellion or the desire to fit in.

However, I was keenly aware that Mam would not tolerate such behaviour if she knew.  Mam had instilled in me a strong sense of right and wrong, and I knew that crossing certain lines would result in swift and severe consequences.  Despite this knowledge, I was frequently in trouble with my teachers, particularly those who taught academic subjects.

It wasn't that I sought trouble intentionally; in fact, I often found myself simply caught up in situations where my friends' antics landed me in hot water.  Whether it was skipping class, talking back to teachers, disrupting class or failing to complete homework on time, I was continually on the receiving end of reprimands and punishments more often than I cared to admit.

I knew that this behaviour was not in line with the values Mam had instilled in me.  I felt a sting of guilt each time I was in trouble, knowing that I was disappointing myself and would disappoint Mam if she knew.  However, the need to fit in with my peers and the excitement of breaking the rules proved difficult to resist.

As the school year progressed, I was at a crossroads. I knew that continuing down this path would only lead to more trouble and disappointment.  With reluctance I began to distance myself from my wayward friends, choosing instead to focus on my studies and my future.

As I navigated my teenage years, my behaviour at home began to take a concerning turn.  Regardless of my efforts to focus on my schoolwork and improve my

behaviour, I became increasingly difficult to manage.  I
started arriving home late without explanation,
answering Mam back, and even occasionally swearing,
behaviour that was completely out of character for the
daughter that Mam knew and loved.

Mam was at a loss as she witnessed this change in
me.  She tried to understand what might be causing the
sudden change in my behaviour, searching for clues or
signs of distress.  Raising a teenager was never easy, and
Mam knew that confrontations and challenges were a
normal part of the process.  However, she couldn't shake
the feeling of unease as she watched me become
increasingly defiant and unmanageable.

Adding to Mam's frustration was the lack of support
she felt from Grandad.  While Mam tried to approach the
situation with understanding and patience, Grandad often
resorted to threats and telling me off, believing that
tough love was the answer to my rebellious behaviour.
Unfortunately, this only seemed to exacerbate the
situation as I reacted with defiance and resentment to his
attempts to control me.

Mam knew that threatening me would only lead to
further rebellion and resentment.  Instead, she tried to
approach the situation with empathy and compassion,
hoping to uncover the root cause of my behaviour and to
address it together as a family.  Despite the challenges
she faced, Mam remained determined to support me

through this difficult time.  She knew that I needed love, understanding and guidance more than ever, and she was willing to do whatever it took to help me journey through this tumultuous period of adolescence.

Mam felt the world crumbling around her.  The loss of Nana had left a profound emptiness in her heart.  Nana had been more than a parent.  She had been Mam's mainstay, her guiding light through life's tumultuous times.  Without her steady presence, Mam felt lost, struggling to deal with the challenges of single parenthood while also bearing the weight of her own grief.

At that age, I never truly understood the impact that Nana's death had had on the family.  It wasn't until much later in life that I began to really feel the enormity of loss and the gaping void it had left in Mam's life.  Mam and Nana had shared a bond that exceeded simple family ties; theirs was a relationship filled with devotion for each other very rarely experienced in a family unit.  As a child, I witnessed their closeness, but it was only after my own Mam's death that I truly began to comprehend the depth of their connection and what it meant to Mam to lose it.

Losing Mam was like being robbed of my steady rock that had supported me through life's hard times for fifty-two years.  Facing the empty expanse of grief, I came to realise that while my husband had vowed to stand by me, his support was barely noticeable and he could never fill the void left by Mam's absence.  Despite having a husband and a family of my own, the pain of her loss cut deep, leaving me feeling alone and vulnerable.

I look back at my adolescent times, knowing now how alone and vulnerable she, too, must have been feeling and seeing now that my behaviour wasn't helping.

As if that wasn't enough, Grandad had seemingly given up on life.  His decision to stop working only added to the financial strain on the household, leaving Mam as the sole breadwinner.  Even more distressing was Grandad's decline into apathy and lethargy.  He seemed to have lost all interest in the world around him, spending his days sitting by the fire, smoking his Parkies, and forgetting even the simplest of tasks.

Mam felt the weight of responsibility crashing down on her shoulders, threatening to suffocate her with its sheer magnitude.  She juggled the demands of work, household chores and my emotional needs, all while grappling with her own grief and exhaustion.

During the chaotic period of caring for Grandad and managing adolescence, Mam decided to instil a sense of responsibility in me by giving me weekly housekeeping duties.  Every Friday afternoon, upon returning home, I was expected to clean the downstairs rooms.  This wasn't just a matter of a quick tidy-up; it was a thorough cleaning, from sweeping and mopping the lino floors to dusting the furniture and cherished knick-knacks on the sideboard.  Even the front doorstep received the scrubbing brush treatment.

I was never able to complete the cleaning before Mam returned from work, despite all my efforts, and then she still expected the task to be finished before dinner.  Adding a touch of irony to the chore, Mam would rate my cleaning efforts on a scale of one to ten.  Much to my frustration, I never received a perfect score, which left me wondering what more I could do to achieve top marks.  In moments of annoyance, I would appeal to Mam, asking what I had to do to get a perfect score.  Mam's response was simple although profound:

"If I give you a 10, that means you've done a perfect job, and nobody is perfect."

I struggled to understand Mam's explanation because I felt confident in my cleaning abilities.  In hindsight, I came to realise that perfection isn't always possible, and true success lies in the effort put forward rather than in the pursuit of perfection.  Through Mam's housekeeping example, I learned valuable lessons in humility, perseverance, and the acceptance of imperfection.

Mam refused to give in to despair, despite the overwhelming challenges she faced. She drew strength from the memory of her mother's endurance and determination, knowing that she had inherited those same qualities. She tackled each day head-on, with constant resolve, determined to provide for her family and create a better future for me.

Watching over Grandad, Mam couldn't help but feel a twinge of sadness for the man he had once been: strong, capable, and full of life. But she also knew that she couldn't force him to change. It was as though he had given up on life now that his wife was no longer by his side. Mam could only focus on the things she was able to control and find moments of comfort amidst the chaos.

The tension in the air was tangible as Mam answered the backdoor to find her neighbour, Dottie, standing there, her face twisted in anger. Dottie wasted no time in accusing me of swearing at her when she had dared to reprimand me for my cheekiness and disrespect. Mam's heart sank at what she was hearing. This was the final straw; the breaking point she had been dreading.

In a flash of anger and frustration, Mam screamed for me to come to the door and apologise to Dottie. But instead of compliance, I chose defiance, arguing that Dottie had no right to scold me in the first place. With each word exchanged, tensions escalated until I turned and walked away, leaving Mam seething with rage.

Without a second thought, Mam gave chase, her anger charging her determination to confront me and demand I take responsibility.  Through the house, out of the front door, and into the street we went, Mam's desperate pleas falling on deaf ears as I continued to evade her grasp.  Finally, after a frantic pursuit up and down the entryway, and in and out of the back door several times, Mam caught up with me, her fury reaching its boiling point.  With a rapid motion of rage, she removed her slipper and began to administer swift punishment, delivering a sharp whack to my bottom with each step I took up the stairs.

Overwhelmed by shame and regret, I sobbed uncontrollably as Mam's discipline rained down upon me.  The reality of my actions hit me like a bolt of lightning, leading me to realise the pain and hurt I had caused Mam.

Mam's anger gave way to sadness as she instructed me to go to my room and remain there until I was told otherwise.  It was a punishment given out of love and desperation, a last resort in the face of defiance and disobedience.

Retreating to my room, I was so scared that Mam would never be able to forgive me.  I vowed to myself to do better, to make amends for my mistakes and to rebuild the trust and respect that had been fractured by my actions.  And as I lay in bed, tears rolling down my cheeks, I knew that the road ahead would be long and difficult, but I was determined to make things right.

My resolve never to push Mam again to the point of losing control remained firm in my mind.  I knew the pain I had caused and vowed never to let my actions bring such anguish upon her again.  Though there were many moments when I tested my luck, I recognised the line and stopped short, unwilling to impose further distress upon my beautiful, tolerant Mam.

As for school, I started to take on new responsibilities and tasks that I had never been entrusted with before.  Rather than shying away from the challenge, I embraced it wholeheartedly, seeing it as an opportunity to display my strengths and prove myself capable.  With each task I completed, I felt a sense of accomplishment and pride, knowing that I was making progress and earning the respect of my teachers and my peers.

# Twenty-five

*T*he change in me was nothing short of remarkable. Where there had once been defiance and recklessness, there was now maturity and responsibility. Looking towards the future, I knew that the path ahead was back on track, guided by my sense of purpose sparked by my determination to make Mam proud. And with each step forward, I embraced the journey with open arms, ready to seize every opportunity.

My efforts did not go unnoticed. At the end of the school year, I was awarded a royal blue sash to wear around my gym slip, a symbol of my appointment as a prefect for my final year. The recognition filled me with validation and pride, confirming my sense of purpose and direction. I stepped into my final year of schooling at the age of 14 and embraced the added responsibilities presented to me as a school prefect with enthusiasm and gratitude. I was so proud to wear my royal-blue sash and my prefect badge and saw them as a proof of my growth and maturity, thankful that my teachers had recognised my potential and entrusted me with such important roles.

I remained focused on my studies but found that the practical subjects truly stood out to me during my final year. In needlework class, I poured my creativity and attention to detail into making a dressing gown, relishing the opportunity to showcase my skills and craftsmanship.

Similarly, in cookery class, I found satisfaction in experimenting with different recipes and techniques. From savoury dishes to delectable desserts, I threw myself into the culinary arts with enjoyment, eager to expand my repertoire and perfect my skills. I made my first Christmas Cake at school and it became a firm favourite with the family members who would join us at Christmas, earning me praise and admiration from all.

As the school year progressed, I contemplated my future career path. Determined not to settle for a menial job like a factory worker or shop assistant, I yearned for something more substantial, something that would offer room for advancement and personal growth.

One evening, Grandad and I were scouring the job vacancy pages of the Leicester Mercury and stumbled upon an interesting opportunity at Marshall and Snelgrove Department Store in Gallowtree Gate. The advertisement sought a young female, preferably a forthcoming school leaver, to undergo training as a Comptometer Operator in their Statistics office.

I hesitated, voicing my lack of confidence in my maths skills, but Grandad swiftly dismissed my doubts, insisting I had the potential to stand out in the role. It was a form of support I had never experienced from him before, and it was very gratifying.

Mam arrived home from work. I wasted no time in sharing the details of the advertisement, my enthusiasm shining through despite lingering doubts about my mathematical abilities.

I needed Mam's opinion and reassurance. She was quick to offer her support and guidance. Without hesitation, she encouraged me to approach the school the next day with a request for time off to explore the job opportunity further. Her swift and decisive response filled me with a renewed confidence as I prepared to take the next step in my journey towards a fulfilling career.

I spoke to my teacher the following morning about being able to go to the department store to see about the opportunity of employment there. The school's commitment to help students find work meant that I was able to prioritise my job search. With permission granted to take a few hours off, I left the school premises, still clad in my uniform, and set off on the lengthy walk to the store.

From the opposite side of the street I noticed the elegant façade of Marshall and Snelgrove Department Store and I thought to myself, this is really posh! Following the advertisement's instructions, I approached the well-dressed doorman and politely asked for directions to the Administration Manager's office.  He kindly directed me to the lift where an assistant was waiting to guide me to the correct floor and office.  I was so excited!  Every moment of this experience felt surreal and exhilarating.

In the confines of the lift, my mind raced with thoughts of what securing a job at Marshall and Snelgrove could mean for me.  The prestige associated with the establishment filled me with a sense of pride.  I imagined the admiration I would get from others, and the pride Mam would undoubtedly feel at my success.

Miss Blackshaw greeted me at the office manager's door, a smartly dressed woman wearing a tight skirt and towering high heels, a sight uncommon in my usual surroundings.  Despite my initial nerves, I found myself drawn to her welcoming manner.

Seated across from each other, Miss Blackshaw initiated a conversation that extended beyond the job description, expressing genuine interest in me.  As our discussion neared its conclusion, the manager mentioned that a decision would be deferred until the advert's expiry date had been reached.  She also mentioned the need for a character reference from my school and the possibility of a maths test as part of the application process.

My confidence wavered at the mention of a maths test.  Doubts crept in as I worried about my academic history and whether my school would provide a favourable reference.  Despite my sudden apprehension, I maintained my composure, expressing my thanks to Miss Blackshaw for the opportunity.

As I left the office, I couldn't stop the nagging uncertainty looming over me.  How would I fare in a maths test?  What would my school say about me?  Despite these doubts, I would definitely face the challenge head-on, determined to prove myself worthy of the opportunity that lay before me.

Two weeks had passed since my meeting with Miss Blackshaw.  Each afternoon, after completing my paper round, I hurried home, eager to check for any sign of news.  At long last, my eyes caught sight of a long brown envelope resting on the table in the living room.  I longed to share this moment with Mam, but Grandad's eagerness proved contagious.  Unable to contain my curiosity any longer, I tore open the envelope, revealing an official-looking letter bearing Miss Blackshaw's signature at the bottom.

The letter confirmed my invitation to undertake a maths test, a crucial step in determining my suitability for the job.  The weight of the moment settled upon my shoulders as I absorbed the implications of the test's outcome.  The letter also explained that a decision would be made promptly following the assessment, sparing me from any further agonising wait.

I felt a surge of determination to succeed and prepared myself for the challenge ahead, ready to face the test head-on.

I was seated nervously in Miss Blackshaw's office again, this time accompanied by another candidate. Though we sat apart, I could sense that the other girl was as tense as I was. However, my nerves soon dissipated as I realised that the maths test primarily comprised basic arithmetic: addition, subtraction, multiplication and division. There were a few mental arithmetic questions thrown in, but I was relieved to find no fractions or percentages in sight.

Completing the test almost simultaneously with the other candidate, I handed my papers to Miss Blackshaw's secretary. With nothing left to do but wait, my fingers were crossed and my mind raced with hope.

Eventually, I was summoned to face Miss Blackshaw for the results. I had come this far and now stood on the point of securing the desirable role of Comptometer Operator in the Statistics office. Miss Blackshaw wasted no time in delivering the news. She congratulated me on successfully navigating the interview process and expressed her eagerness for me to join the team. Overwhelmed with gratitude, I thanked

Miss Blackshaw then hurried home to share the good news with Grandad.

Instead of waiting for Mam to return from work, I made a spontaneous visit to her factory and climbed the stairs to her floor.  I was greeted by a chorus of excitement from Mam and her colleagues, all eagerly awaiting news of the interview.  Bursting with joy, I exclaimed,

"I've got it!"  Mam and her workmates engulfed me in hugs and congratulations, celebrating my well-deserved success.

I returned to school the following day, only to find myself summoned to see the headmistress, Mrs. Richardson.  Oh dear, this wasn't good.  My elated heart sank.  I wracked my brain for any wrongdoing I might have committed, though I couldn't recall anything significant.

To my surprise, I was greeted with a warm smile while Mrs Richardson began by extending her congratulations.  Miss Blackshaw had contacted the school to inform her of my successful application for the job.  However, Mrs. Richardson had more to share.

In a touching gesture, she commended me for my significant change over the past 18 months, noting my dedication and hard work.  She announced that I would be awarded the prize for Best Overall Achiever at the end-of-year assembly.  I sat in stunned silence, trying to keep grasp of the whirlwind of events unfolding around me.  It felt as though my world was changing at a dizzy pace, and I could hardly believe the incredible opportunities that were coming my way.

On the final day of term, I stood before the school and received the award for Best Overall Achiever.  My prize was a hard-backed copy of Louisa May Alcott's 'Little Women'.  Pride swelled within me as I accepted the recognition.  Yet, beneath the surface, I also felt a pang of sorrow as I bid farewell to my friends.  The end of the school year marked the sad closing of one chapter in my life and the exciting beginning of another.

On Monday, July 9th, 1962, just nine days before my 15th birthday, I began the next stage of my journey: my working life.  With a mix of apprehension and anticipation, I stepped into the unknown, ready to embrace the challenges and adventures that lay ahead. The world was brimming with possibilities, and I stood poised to seize them all.

# Twenty-six

Despite the glimmer of hope brought about by my new employment, life at home remained shrouded in challenges for everyone.  While financial restraints lessened slightly, the burden of caring for Grandad who was now in the throes of early dementia was another worry on Mam's already overladen shoulders.

As signs of Grandad's condition became more noticeable, Mam found herself wrestling with the increasing demands of care giving.  His memory lapses and bouts of confusion created a constant state of anxiety, with Mam often having to intervene to ensure his safety.  However, there was always the risk of him wandering disoriented through the streets.

For a young teenager witnessing these changes, understanding Grandad's erratic behaviour proved to be a difficult task.  Frustration and impatience mounted as his demands and complaints added tension to the household dynamics.  Simple tasks became hard work.  He struggled with meals, noise, and basic concepts, further exacerbating the already challenging environment.

The strain on Mam was evident.  What was once a harmonious home now felt fraught with tension, overshadowed by the realities of Grandad's decline.  Even with our best efforts to maintain stability and nurture a sense of normality, each day became a struggle amidst the chaos.

Mam's feelings of guilt increased as she guided Grandad to the doctor's surgery.  His decline in mental health and the increasing challenges with incontinence had become burdens too heavy for her to bear alone.  With a deep breath, Mam sought help.  The doctor listened attentively to her concerns, offering medical advice and support.  Then, a seemingly unexpected question arose:

"Do you have a television at home?"  Mam shook her head, puzzled by the enquiry.

"No, we don't," she replied.  A thoughtful look crossed the doctor's face as he leaned forward.

"When it's financially possible, having a TV might help Albert," he suggested.  "Watching television can be an enjoyable way to pass the time and provide stimulation, especially for someone with early-onset dementia."

Mam pondered the doctor's suggestion long after they had left the surgery, the idea lingering in her mind like a persistent whisper.  Despite our limited finances, Mam resolved to heed the advice and bring a glimmer of entertainment into our humble home so she embarked on a quest to find a solution.  After careful consideration, she settled on renting a black and white television, a modest yet significant step towards brightening our lives.

One crisp Saturday morning, Mam ventured to the Rediffusion Television shop on Belgrave Gate, feeling quite anxious.  Television was something she didn't understand, she didn't know whether it would work for Grandad and it would cost her money.  The warm greeting from the shopkeeper eased her nerves and she explained her situation with sincerity.  Together, they selected a modest television set that would fit snugly in the living room, one she could afford at 8 shillings a week (40p in today's money).

As she left the shop, Mam felt relieved.  She may not have solved all our problems but had taken a step forward.  She hoped that a TV in our home would bring a spark of joy to us all, especially into Grandad's life, a small comfort in the face of his rising confusion.

The much-awaited day arrived when the television set was delivered and installed.  Excitement filled the air as we all gathered around the TV, admiring the huge 21-inch screen, encased in a large wooden cabinet.

Grandad settled comfortably in his chair with his cigarettes and ashtray perched nearby, especially eager to experience the marvel of television technology.  With bated breath, we waited, eyes fixed on the screen.  With a flick of the switch, the screen came to life, and we were all immediately drawn to the images flickering before us.  The television had a mesmerising effect, holding our attention like never before.  As time passed, the TV became an indispensable part of our daily routine.  Grandad found amusement and enjoyment in programmes such as 'Steptoe and Son', allowing him to focus on the present moment and forget about his troubles, if only for a few hours..

After supper each evening, Grandad insisted on staying up until the national anthem played and the white dot in the middle of the screen disappeared, signalling the end of the day's broadcast, usually between 10.30pm and midnight.  Only then would he reluctantly agree to switch off the TV and retire for the night.

Our home became a place of shared experiences and cherished moments, much like countless others across the nation.  The traditional strains of the national anthem served as a unifying power, bringing families together in front of their screens, no matter how far apart they may be.

I was intrigued by the arrival of the television and easily drawn to its attraction.  However, Grandad had his own program preferences, which often occupied the screen in the evenings.  Respecting his wishes, I retreated to the front room, losing myself in the sounds of my favourite music selected from my record collection.

As the nights wore on, a worrying pattern emerged. Mam would often come downstairs in the morning to find Grandad fast asleep in his chair, the television still casting its faint glow, though now silent. It was also a concern to find the sight of a half-burned cigarette left in the ashtray.

Fearful for Grandad's safety, Mam talked to him about her worries. She gently explained the dangers of leaving cigarettes unattended or falling asleep with a cigarette in his hand. A decision was made to remove them each night before she went to bed. It was a small but necessary precaution, ensuring we could all sleep safely without the worrying fear of a potential fire.

The television brought an element of joy and a new routine to our lives. For Grandad, it offered welcome enjoyment and distraction, while I found enjoyment in my music. And though our evenings were filled with different interests, we remained united in our concern for each other.

I acknowledged my share of responsibility in the house, and dutifully contributed to the family finances by paying Mam weekly for my board. Even with my willingness to support my family, the overall financial burden was Mam's responsibility. With my grandad no longer able to work, the family's income had taken a significant hit. My earnings of £7 a week allowed me the opportunity to buy clothes and shoes and any luxuries such as records (singles and LPs) but it was still a delicate balancing act for Mam to manage the household budget.  Despite my contribution of £3 a week, Mam had to apply caution and careful planning to make ends meet.  Every penny was stretched and accounted for, guaranteeing that essentials were prioritised and unnecessary expenses were minimised.

Each Friday evening, as the week drew to a close, Mam returned home from work, weary but determined.  With a steaming cup of tea in hand, she began her weekly ritual: sorting the household income into small tins labelled for their designated purposes.  She methodically allocated shillings for the rent, carefully counted out coins for the gas and electric meters and set aside funds for life insurance.  The food money and any savings were kept together and anything left over would help towards any holidays in the future.  Like clockwork, the insurance man would arrive, a regular visitor seeking his collection.

But life's uncertainties sometimes disrupted Mam's carefully laid plans.  If she found herself short of funds one week, it was the life insurance tins that bore the brunt.  Feeling guilty, she would draw the curtains and ensure silence reigned as the insurance man knocked on the door, eventually departing, none the wiser.

Mam remained firm in her principles.  Every penny she allocated was a credit to her consistent effort to securing the home, warmth, and food for her family: Grandad, herself and me. My contribution, though modest, served as a lifeline for Mam, relieving some of the financial strain and allowing us to manage our circumstances with greater stability and hope.

During the summer of 1963, Mam and I found ourselves in a position we had never been in before. We were working tirelessly, and our hard work was finally paying off. Mam, in particular, had reason to celebrate. She had been promoted to the position of forewoman at the factory where she worked. This new role came with added responsibilities as she would now oversee the workers on the factory floor. She had to ensure quality control was at its best and that the workers operated at maximum efficiency. As a reward for her dedication and hard work, Mam was now on staff wages, providing her with a new-found sense of security and a welcome boost to her weekly pay packet.

Meanwhile, after a year of loyal dedication, I had achieved the status of a fully-fledged comptometer operator. This milestone not only brought me immense personal satisfaction but also came with a promotion. Recognising that I was now an experienced operator, a large increase in salary came with the it, adding a welcome boost to my family's financial security.

Mam and I were proud of ourselves. The determination that we had poured into our work had unlocked doors to opportunities that once seemed out of reach, enriching our lives in ways we had only dared to imagine.

As the months went by, Mam's concern for Grandad's well-being grew. It wasn't just his forgetfulness that troubled her, but the gradual decline in his ability to take care of himself. Simple tasks like dressing became increasingly difficult for him, and he was struggling with incontinence more frequently.

This was a distressing situation for Mam. Not only did she witness the effects of senility taking a toll on Grandad, but she also questioned the implications it had on our home environment. As his condition worsened, Mam couldn't help but worry about the embarrassment he faced, often being found without his clothes on and smelling unpleasant.

Mam faced the heart-breaking realisation that her father's dignity was slipping away and she struggled with the emotional weight of it all. Although Mam understood that Grandad was unwell, there were moments when her empathy couldn't fully shield her from feeling embarrassed by his appearance and the challenges his condition brought into our lives.

Mam wrestled with conflicting emotions, her love and concern for Grandad clashing with her own discomfort and distress. It was a difficult journey for both of them, navigating the complexities of ageing and illness while trying to preserve dignity and maintain a sense of normality in their lives.

One day, a few weeks later, Mam received a call from Tommy Cox, the local baker, while she was at work.  His urgent tone immediately set off alarm bells in her mind.  Tommy informed Mam that he had spotted Grandad walking along Wharf Street wearing nothing but his pyjama bottoms, with no shoes on his feet.  The news hit Mam hard, her worst fears had come true.  Grandad, in a state of confusion, had wandered out of the house alone, oblivious to his surroundings and his lack of appropriate clothing.  Without a moment's hesitation, Mam abandoned her tasks at work and dashed out onto the street.  Every step she took felt like an eternity as panic ran through her veins.  Images of Grandad, vulnerable and disoriented, haunted her thoughts.  She couldn't bear the idea of him wandering the streets alone, exposed to danger and humiliation.

Finally reaching Wharf Street, Mam examined the area frantically, her eyes searching for any sign of Grandad.  And then, in the crowd, she spotted him, her dear father, bewildered and lost, shuffling along in his pyjama bottoms.  With a surge of relief mixed with worry, Mam hurried towards him, holding him in a tight embrace.  Tears welled up in her eyes as she held him close, grateful to have found him safe but shaken by the realisation of how vulnerable he truly was.

There and then, Mam made a solemn vow never to leave Grandad alone again, to protect him and ensure that he received the care and attention he needed to live out his days in dignity and safety. And as they made their way back home, hand in hand, Mam knew that she would do whatever it took to keep her promise.

Mam now found herself at a crossroads, unsure of which path to take. Balancing the demands of her full-time job at the factory with the increasing needs of Grandad seemed an impossible task. Feeling overwhelmed and desperate for guidance, she decided to seek help from the doctor's surgery. Recognising the gravity of the situation, the doctor arranged for Grandad to undergo a thorough assessment by the local mental health team.

Within days, Grandad was assessed, and the results were sobering. The mental health doctor advised Mam that, for Grandad's own safety and well-being, he would be better off in a care home for the elderly where he could receive round-the-clock attention and support.

The news hit Mam like a ton of bricks. She was devastated by the realisation that she could no longer provide the level of care Grandad needed on her own. Guilt gnawed at her conscience as she grappled with the difficult decision ahead.  She had always promised herself that she would look after Grandad until the end, just has she had done for Nana six years earlier, but now she faced the painful truth that circumstances had forced her hand.  Despite the overwhelming sense of guilt and sadness, Mam knew that she had to prioritise Grandad's safety above all else.  She made the agonising decision to place him in a care home, knowing that it was the best option for his safety, that she was doing what was necessary to ensure Grandad's quality of life.  And though the decision was a difficult one, she knew that she had to put both herself and me first in order to provide the best possible care for Grandad in his time of need.

Mam's heart sank with dread, however, as she contemplated where Grandad might be placed for his future care.  There was one place she prayed he wouldn't end up: Hillcrest Hospital on Swain Street.  The mere thought sent shivers down her spine.

Hillcrest Hospital held a dark and dismal reputation, rooted in its past as the Leicester workhouse.  Stories of the workhouse circulated among the neighbours, often accompanied by grim reviews.  Even now, with its transformation into a hospital, Mam couldn't shake the haunting image of the building from her mind.  The very mention of Hillcrest Hospital conjured up images of desolation and despair.  Mam had heard tales of the harsh conditions and strict regime that once characterised the workhouse.  Even though times had changed, the building itself retained an aura of gloom and she couldn't bear the thought of Grandad being confined to such a place, surrounded by the echoes of past suffering.  She longed for him to receive care in a setting that was warm, welcoming and healing, not one that carried the weight of its troubled history.

Despite her fears, Mam knew that, ultimately, the decision was out of her hands.  She could only hope and pray that Grandad would be placed in a facility where he would be treated with compassion and dignity, far away from the shadows of Hillcrest Hospital on Swain Street.

A few days later, the dreaded letter arrived, confirming Grandad's placement at Hillcrest Hospital. Mam became engulfed in a whirlwind of emotions.  With no other possible options and the weight of her job pressing down on her, Mam knew she had little choice but to accept the council's decision.  The letter extended an invitation for Mam to visit the hospital and see the facilities first hand, perhaps in an effort to ease her apprehension.  Reluctantly, Mam agreed, knowing that she needed to come to terms with the reality of the situation.

The following Saturday morning, Mam, Grandad, and I made our way to Hillcrest Hospital.  Grandad, still grappling with the fog of confusion that often accompanied his condition, didn't fully comprehend what was happening.  Nevertheless, Mam felt it was important for him to be involved in the decision-making process, no matter how limited his understanding.

As we stepped through the doors of Hillcrest, Mam's heart was lightened by the surprise of what greeted her inside.  The interior was a far cry from the gloomy image she had conjured up in her mind.  The hospital was clean, well-lit, and exuded a sense of warmth.  The staff members we encountered were friendly and welcoming, putting Mam's anxieties somewhat at ease.

We walked through the corridors and explored the various facilities.  Mam couldn't help but feel a sense of relief.  While Hillcrest wasn't perfect, it was certainly better than she had imagined.  The rooms were comfortable, the amenities adequate and, most importantly, the environment felt safe and nurturing.  As we left Hillcrest that day, Mam couldn't help but feel a glimmer of hope amidst the uncertainty, knowing that Grandad would be in good hands.  Within a week of receiving the confirmation letter, Grandad was admitted to Hillcrest Hospital.  Mam and I accompanied him on his journey, apprehensive about how he would settle in yet hopeful that he would find comfort in his new surroundings.

The small ward of four beds that would become Grandad's home was a cosy space, furnished with just enough to accommodate his clothes and personal belongings.  Mam carefully placed a few pictures of Nana, herself and me on the windowsill next to Grandad's bed, hoping to bring him some everyday comfort amidst the unfamiliarity of his new environment.  Even with the rapid progression of his condition, Grandad still retained the precious ability to recognise us, a blessing that Mam and I cherished deeply.  It was a small consolation for the position that we found ourselves in.

Once Grandad was settled into his room, we were invited to join the other residents and their families in the dining area for a cup of tea.  Saturday afternoon visiting hours brought a sense of warmth and sociability as families gathered to spend time together.

Mam and I mingled with the other visitors.  I couldn't help but notice one of the orderlies, a young man with a friendly smile and a kind demeanour.  I felt inexplicably drawn to him.  It was a new and warm sensation, the prospect of attraction stirring.

The orderly made his rounds with the tea trolley, offering tea and biscuits to the residents and our eyes met.  I felt a spark of connection that sent a thrill through me.  Though I had never experienced a romantic advance before, something in his gaze hinted at a mutual attraction, igniting a flutter of excitement within me. The glance from the hospital orderly lingered in my mind like an echo, leaving me questioning its significance.  Was he truly looking at me with a soft smile, or was it just a fleeting moment of imagination?

The encounter stirred a whirlwind of emotions and self-reflection.  I had yet to experience the intricacies of young love, the desire for acceptance foremost in my mind.  The idea of having a boyfriend seemed like an opportunity of hope, a chance to showcase my worth and find a sense of belonging.

As I had never considered myself as being slim, my confidence in my appearance was minimal, overshadowed by insecurities that had long plagued my thoughts.  However, the simple glance from the orderly ignited an awareness of my desire to present myself in a favourable light, especially when visiting Grandad.  I was determined to try to look nice for my visits to the hospital as it wasn't just about Grandad anymore; it was about reclaiming a sense of self-worth and confidence in my own skin.

# Twenty-seven

*E*xcitement filled the air in the early autumn of 1963 as Mam and I prepared for our first journey abroad. Mam had carefully arranged a bus tour to Belgium and Holland, eager to share in the experience of exploring new lands and creating cherished memories together.

I was sixteen and delighted by the freedom of being able to purchase fashionable clothes with my own hard-earned money. The prospect of travelling abroad was huge and sparked a need to present myself in the best possible light. If one person had shown an interest in me before, perhaps others would too, especially if I looked my best!

There was a distinct feeling of freedom in the air as we packed our suitcases and prepared for the journey ahead. There were no responsibilities weighing us down, no obligations to attend to other than our jobs. It was a rare opportunity to escape the routine of daily life and immerse ourselves in the thrill of adventure. This was our first taste of freedom!

We met the bus at Humberstone Gate. Before leaving, we proudly presented our brand-new passports as the two bus drivers carefully checked each one and ensured we had everything we needed for the week ahead. It was a journey of discovery, not only of new places but also of the bond shared between a mother and daughter.

Our senses were overwhelmed by the energetic activity of the ferry terminal at Dover that night, with the sight of cars boarding huge ferry boats, and the reflection of the boats shimmering in the water, their lights casting a mesmerising glow. It was a scene straight out of a dream and we hadn't even left England yet. Now, aboard the ferry, we left the relaxation of the bus behind and ascended the stairs to the boat deck feeling the salty breeze whistling through our hair as we found our seats. Everything was so different to anything I had ever experienced before. I was filled with wonder and disbelief. Was this really happening to me? We couldn't help but feel it very surreal.

It was the beginning of a new chapter, a gateway to adventure that promised to take us to places we had only ever dreamed of. My first surprise was the absence of light. I had never truly experienced darkness quite like this. The ferry was slicing through the English Channel, leaving Dover's docks and white cliffs shrinking in the distance, while the port of Ostend remained elusive. As the separation between land and sea widened, I found myself engulfed in an abyss of darkness that seemed to stretch endlessly. Apart from various sources of light scattered across the vessel, we were surrounded by a thick blackness where the only audible reminder of the world outside was the haunting sound of waves crashing against the unseen hull of the boat.  It all felt very strange, stirring an eerie feeling within me.  And as I stood there, a mere speck in the vast expanse of the night, I realised just how small and insignificant we are in the universe.

Dawn painted the horizon with a delicate palette of soft pastel shades as we headed towards the ferry terminal in Ostend.  We were both tired.  We had had little chance of any rest.  However, the prospect of our first glimpse of a foreign land kept us awake and alert.

We strained our eyes to catch our first glimpse of Ostend.  Surprisingly, the scene that greeted us bore a striking resemblance to the one we had left behind in Dover some six hours before.  Ferry boats, their lights still aglow, dotted the waters, while clusters of cranes stood by the docks, their towering frames casting long shadows in the early morning light.  Back on dry land, the bus made its first stop at a nearby service area and we were curious to see what a Belgian breakfast had to offer.  While a cup of tea was a familiar choice, the rest of the menu was a delightful change from our usual English breakfast offering.

Instead of the eggs, bacon and beans that we were accustomed to, the offerings at the service area leaned towards a more continental choice.  Plates full of freshly baked croissants, assorted meats, and cheeses greeted us, presenting a tempting array of flavours and textures.

It was a culinary adventure unlike any we had experienced before. The simplicity of the Belgian breakfast reminded us of a bygone era, where morning meals were less about quantity and more about tasting the delicate flavours of bread, cheese, and jams. Sitting down to enjoy our meal, eating thin waffles served with slices of cheese or a serving of jam, we couldn't help but appreciate already the charm of Belgian cuisine.

Our first destination was Brussels, Belgium's capital city. We stepped foot onto the cobbled streets and entered a world of entirely unfamiliar customs and traditions. Everything around us seemed to beat with the vibrancy of a culture we had only seen in books and films.

The architecture in the Grand Place spoke of a rich history, with ornate buildings decorated with intricate carvings and colourful façades. Mam and I wandered through the bustling streets, our senses awakened by a symphony of sights, sounds, and smells. The language, a melodic blend of French and Dutch, floated through the air, mingling with the inviting aromas wafting from nearby bakeries and cafes. Market stalls overflowed with unusual fruits and vegetables, their strong aromas an example of the diversity of the local cuisine. Craftsmen steadily applied their trade, crafting intricate lace and delicate chocolates, each creation a masterpiece in its own right.

Every corner we turned in Brussels revealed a new discovery, each one more enchanting than the last. We found the iconic Manneken Pis, a cheeky statue of a naked little boy relieving himself into the fountain's basin. It was petite in size, but it exuded a charm that captured the hearts of passers-by and tourists alike. Moving on, we stumbled upon a lively festival celebrating the very essence of Belgian culture. From frothy beers to succulent mussels, the air was alive with the infectious energy of visitors indulging in the country's culinary treats.

Wandering through Brussels' beautiful Galleries, we were attracted by the colourful ambiance that filled the air. Cafes buzzed with laughter while street musicians serenaded crowds of people, adding to the city's dynamic atmosphere.

And then there were the shop windows, each one a tantalising display of Belgium's most famous export: chocolate. Row after row of confectionery delights beckoned to us, their rich aromas and decadent flavours tempting us to indulge in their irresistible sweetness. How could we resist?

Mam and I became truly immersed in a world unlike
any we had ever known.  Brussels unfolded before us
like a storybook coming to life.

Our next destination was Ghent, a mere 35 miles
away through picturesque countryside.  We arrived just
as darkness began to descend.  Even under the cover of
night, the town was a vision of enchantment.  The
twinkling lights of its quaint shops illuminated the
cobblestone streets with a warm and inviting glow but it
was the sight of the river that truly took my breath away.
Its tranquil waters mirrored the beauty of the
surrounding buildings, creating a shimmering
simplicity of light and shadow that danced upon its
surface.  Ghent looked like somewhere out of a fairy
tale, a hidden gem waiting to be discovered.

The bus made a stop at a beautiful restaurant close to
the quiet riverbank.  A meal had been arranged for us to
savour, and savour we certainly did.  The air was alive
with the tempting smells of freshly prepared dishes,
promising a culinary experience unlike any other.
Seated at a table overlooking the gently flowing river,
Mam and I were presented with a feast for the taste buds.
Each dish that graced our table was a masterpiece in its
own right, a mixture of flavours and textures that
delighted our palates with every bite.  From delicate
seafood dishes to hearty local specialities, we loved each

mouthful, allowing ourselves to be transported on a gastronomic journey unlike any we had been on before.

Dining beneath the soft glow of the restaurant's lighting, surrounded by the tranquil beauty of the river, it was a moment of pure extravagance, a culinary dream come true, a memory that would linger in my heart long after the last bite had been tasted.

We explored this enchanting town the following day before boarding the bus that evening for our short journey to Bruges, another destination both Mam and I were looking forward to very much.

Bruges was renowned for its timeless charm and medieval architecture, and we couldn't wait to explore its quaint streets and attractive canals. We were delighted when its spires and rooftops came into view. The following morning, we ventured forth from our hotel into the heart of the city and were greeted by a sight straight out of a storybook. Cobblestone streets lined with historic buildings, their fronts decorated with colourful shutters and window boxes filled with blooms stretched out before us. The gentle lapping of the canal waters and the distant chiming of church bells added to the city's timeless beauty.

We set out to explore every corner of Bruges from its bustling market squares to its hidden alleyways. Mam and I wandered through this magical place and couldn't help but marvel at the allure and charm that surrounded us at every turn. Time seemed to stand still, allowing us to immerse ourselves fully in the city's rich history and vibrant culture.

The next part of our journey took us into Holland, each moment bringing forth new wonders. Cities like Rotterdam and The Hague stood as examples to the uniqueness of Holland compared to Belgium.

We ventured into the Dutch countryside and were greeted by another sort of picturesque landscape. Vast stretches of flat terrain covered with lush greenery spread out before us. Canals criss-crossed the scenery, adding to its attraction, while majestic windmills stood tall, their blades cutting through the air with elegant precision.

In the towns, a different ambience captured us. The Dutch cities, especially The Hague, breathed an industrialised atmosphere, reflecting their roles as busy centres of commerce and governance. Mam and I were in an unending state of amazement, exploring places we had only read about in textbooks during our school days. Were we truly here? We couldn't help but ask ourselves this as we wandered the streets.

One memory stands out vividly in my mind. Mam had the whimsical goal of capturing a moment with a Dutch lady dressed in traditional attire, complete with

the iconic wooden clogs.  Determined to fulfil her wish,
we set out in search of the perfect subject.  It didn't take
long for us to spot an obliging lady, clearly positioned to
cater to eager tourists seeking a slice of Dutch
authenticity, albeit for a fee.

Despite the commercial setup, where tourists were
charged for such snapshots, Mam's focus was solely on
the experience and the memento it would provide.  With
my Brownie 127 camera in hand, I carefully composed
the shot, aiming to immortalise this special moment.  I
couldn't help but wonder if the developed photograph
would truly encapsulate the essence of Mam's delight.

I had envisaged Amsterdam as a city full of bridges
spanning endless canals, with charming buildings lining
the waterways and locals leisurely sipping coffee at
canal-side cafes.  And I wasn't disappointed.  It
surpassed my expectations, its beauty exceeding even
my wildest imagination.  I was overwhelmed with
happiness to know that I would spend my last two days
of this marvellous holiday exploring the enchanting
streets of Amsterdam.

Finally, it was the morning of our departure, and I
felt torn.  I had fallen deeply in love with this city and
the memories Mam and I had made here, but I knew our
visit had come to an end.  Amsterdam would forever
hold a special place in my heart, and I knew I would
cherish the memories of this holiday for a lifetime.

Reluctantly, we boarded our coach and bid farewell to Amsterdam, embarking on the journey back to Belgium.  Our destination for the day was Antwerp, a city of undeniable beauty and charm.  Antwerp's unique culture, a blend of historic and modern, was quintessentially Belgian, and included everything I loved about this country.  From its lively squares to its cosy cafes, every corner of Antwerp seemed to ooze a warmth and hospitality that was truly infectious.  I couldn't help but think about my time in Belgium with fondness.  It was definitely my favourite country.

Our final destination awaited us, Zeebrugge, where we would catch the ferry home.  But as we journeyed onward, my heart remained in Belgium, forever captivated by its beauty and charm.

In the quiet of the bus, something caused me to reflect on the hardships Mam had faced throughout her life.  From the trauma of war to the stigma she endured for having me illegitimately and onto the loss of her mother, her journey had been marked by adversity and sorrow.  Yet, despite the challenges Mam had faced, she had never wavered in her determination to overcome them and to raise me with unconditional love.

My thoughts lingered on the loss of Mam's beloved mother and now her father very poorly, adding to the weight of her burdens.  Her life had been far from easy, a stark contrast to the carefree moments we had just experienced on our holiday.  And yet, here she was, standing tall, her resilience a testament to her strength.

I opened my eyes to her struggles and couldn't help but feel a deep sense of admiration for Mam.  What a woman she was: courageous, resilient, and filled with an unconquerable spirit.  In that moment, I vowed to carry forward her legacy of strength and perseverance, knowing that her example would always guide me through life's challenges.

Upon our return to Leicester after an exhausting journey, we were tired but happy with a multitude of memories to cherish.  The experiences we had shared were like treasures to hold onto, each moment etched into my mind.

The very next day, I rushed to the chemist with the precious film containing 24 exposures.  The wait for the film to be developed felt like an eternity.  Finally, after what seemed like an agonisingly long week, the prints arrived.  I quickly tore open the packet and flipped through the stack of photographs.  To my delight, most of the pictures turned out well, capturing the essence of our journey in vivid detail.

But it was one particular photo that took my breath away, the image of Mam standing beside the Dutch lady, their smiles radiant and genuine.  It was a perfect snapshot of a moment filled with warmth and connection, a memory frozen in time.

That photo, preserved in its perfection, has remained a cherished memento to this day.  It serves as a reminder of the unforgettable journey we had embarked upon and the relationship shared between a mother and her child, exceeding time and distance.  And every time I look at it, I am transported back to that magical time in Holland, reliving the joy and amazement once more.

# Twenty-eight

*T*he Saturday following our return, Mam and I made our usual visit to see Grandad at Hillcrest.  Entering the dining room, his face lit up with a faint recognition, and a smile on his lips.  He still managed to express warmth in his eyes despite his failing memory.

We sat with him for a while, recounting tales of our recent holiday.  However, it soon became apparent that his hold on reality was slipping, and he struggled to follow our conversation.  The doctor had warned us about this, advising us to guide the conversation gently and accept his limitations with patience.

Disappointed to find that the male orderly I had been hoping to see was not on duty, I seized every chance to go and see Grandad again.  The next opportunity presented itself on the following Sunday when Uncle Edward and Auntie Mary arrived for tea, a visit they made most Sunday afternoons.  While they sat chatting with Mam, I took the chance to slip away unnoticed.

With my bicycle at the ready, I made my way to Hillcrest, determined to see the orderly.  I was wandering through the corridors towards Grandad's ward when I spotted him.  His warm smile greeted me, accompanied by a strong Italian accent that I struggled to understand. I greeted him in return, but unfortunately, his response was lost due to the language barrier.  I was determined to communicate with him, even if it meant finding creative ways to bridge the gap between us.

I made my next visit to Grandad on my own as Mam had another appointment to go to.  Sitting beside Grandad, I was slipping into a routine of comforting him, assuring him of Mam's whereabouts, and making him comfortable.  It was a routine I had grown accustomed to, a way to keep him calm and settled, even when his grasp on reality seemed to be disappearing.

The clatter of the tea trolley signalled the entrance of the orderly into the dining room.  I was now familiar with his routine, his presence a must in Grandad's world. He asked Grandad if he would like a biscuit with his tea and Grandad replied,

"Yes please, Tony."

I had now discovered his name.  After he had finished serving tea, Tony approached me, a friendly smile on his face.  He extended an invitation for a cigarette and a chat outside.

I was excited at the prospect of someone taking an interest in me, in sharing a moment away from the dull atmosphere of the nursing home.  Naïve and inexperienced, I eagerly accepted, craving the attention and affection that seemed to escape me elsewhere outside my home.  In that moment, I was willing to follow wherever Tony led, blinded by my desire to feel loved and wanted, and simply just to have a boyfriend!

Communication between Tony and I was difficult. His English was poor and his Italian accent very strong. However, his intentions were clear when he managed to ask me out on a date. It was a simple proposal: a trip to the cinema. I eagerly agreed, thrilled at the prospect of spending more time with him outside the walls of Hillcrest Hospital.

We agreed the time of 7pm the following Wednesday evening at the Savoy Cinema in Belgrave Gate. I could not contain my excitement, though I wondered if Tony was aware of the irony in his choice of film: 'Marriage Italian Style' starring the captivating Sophia Loren. She was an Italian actress renowned for her beauty and, as I found out later, someone Tony admired enormously.

We watched the film together, sharing moments of laughter and quiet contemplation. Despite the language difficulties, there was a sense of connection between us, a shared understanding that exceeded words. As the credits rolled and the lights came up, Tony walked me home, his arm around my waist.

At my doorstep, beneath the soft glow of the street lights, we shared a tentative kiss, a sweet ending to a memorable evening. It was a moment filled with promise, the beginning of something new and exciting, despite the uncertainties that lay ahead.

Mam's excitement mirrored my own. As was our tradition, we shared every detail of my date. Our bond was unbreakable, built on a foundation of trust and open communication. Tonight was no exception. It was a whirlwind of emotions, and for the first time, I understood the sweetness of a kiss, the warmth of affection. Mam could sense my happiness, but she also saw the vulnerability in me, the naivety of a teenager on the brink of new emotions.

Her words of caution were gentle yet firm, a reminder of the realities of life and love.

"Now Anna, you know how to behave, don't you? Don't do anything naughty and end up like I did. Just be careful." Her advice resonated deeply with me, stirring a mix of fear and determination within. I understood the underlying message behind her words, the cautionary tale of the consequences of recklessness. I was scared of facing the same challenges Mam had encountered, of losing myself in the passion without fully understanding the consequences.

I was on the brink of adulthood; now 17, I had my whole life ahead of me. It was a moment of realisation, a turning point where I understood the importance of making wise choices and safeguarding my heart against the pitfalls of love and desire.

Tony and I fell into a routine of seeing each other most evenings.  While we did go out occasionally, most of our time together was spent in the comfort of my front room.  There, on the inviting settee, we found pleasure in each other's company, surrounded by the melodies of my music collection, and particularly the enchanting Italian ballads that Tony had brought along to listen to which soon captured my heart.

As the days turned into weeks, and then months, our friendship deepened.  The simple act of being together, sharing quiet moments and heartfelt conversations, allowed our feelings to blossom and grow stronger.  In the intimacy of those evenings on the settee, it became evident that what we shared was something special, something worth holding onto.  It was a time of joy and a time to discover our emotions and enjoy the simple pleasure of each other's company.  In these tender moments, surrounded by music and wrapped in each other's arms, we found a sense of belonging and contentment that exceeded any words.

A while before I had met Tony, Mam had arranged a surprise holiday for my 18th birthday.  We were to have 10 days in Italy.  The package included a day trip to Venice and Pisa, promising adventures in beautiful locations.

At first, I was delighted at the prospect of another journey abroad with Mam, and the opportunity to explore a new country.  But as my relationship with Tony blossomed, everything changed.  The impending holiday now towered over me with a sense of dread.  How could I possibly enjoy myself when I knew I would be separated from Tony, missing him terribly with each passing moment?

The forthcoming holiday now posed a bittersweet dilemma, torn between the thrill of exploration and the ache of longing for the man I loved.  However, my priority remained clear: to cherish the time with Mam, who had eagerly planned this holiday for us.  I couldn't bear to dampen her excitement with my own feelings, so I hid them, burying the yearning for Tony deep within.

As we made our plans together, organising our itinerary and imagining the adventures that awaited us, the spark of excitement was re-ignited.  The prospect of exploring new places with Mam, creating memories together in beautiful locations, was heavenly.  The holiday would also be an opportunity for me to visit Tony's country of birth, a country he loved and never stopped talking about.

Tony and I had arranged to meet in town the Saturday before my birthday.  We strolled through the busy streets, exploring the shops and enjoying each other's company.  Eventually we found ourselves outside

Bree's Record Store in Churchgate, a quaint shop
near to the iconic Clock Tower.

Excited to browse through the LP (Long Playing)
records, Tony led me downstairs where the collection
awaited.  His intention was to select a special LP as a
birthday gift for me.  However, my mind was
preoccupied with a different concern.  The nagging
worry of a missed period continually plagued my mind,
filling me with anxiety and fear.

With reassurances from my (ill-informed) colleagues
at work that pregnancy didn't happen after the first time,
doubts lingered at the back of my mind.  Was I just being
naive to believe them, or was wishful thinking masking a
deeper concern?  Lost in my thoughts, I absent-mindedly
sifted through the records, my mind consumed by worry.
Suddenly, a wave of dizziness swept over me, and before
I knew it, I had fainted, collapsing to the floor in a heap.
I soon came round and was now sitting on a chair and a
glass of water pressed into my hand.  The concern etched
on Tony's face mirrored my own confusion as I struggled
to understand the sudden turn of events.

I set off home, reassuring Tony that I would be back
soon, masking the upset swirling inside me.  The fear of
missing a period was constantly on my mind, and now
fainting in the record shop added to my worry, but I still
couldn't bring myself to confide in him.  It felt too soon
to start panicking and I clung to the hope that it was just

a passing concern, nothing more.  As I parted ways with Tony, I buried the unsettling thoughts deep within me, determined to push them aside until I had more confirmation.

Mam and I embarked on our long-awaited trip to Italy, filled with excitement for the adventures that lay ahead.  Our destination, the enchanting coastal town of Lido de Jesolo on the Venetian riviera, promising sun-soaked beaches and picturesque views.  We settled into our holiday routine and found ourselves surrounded by a diverse group of holidaymakers, ranging from people my age to older individuals.  Mam, ever sociable, quickly made friends, adding a layer of warmth and togetherness to our journey.

Our days were filled with exploration and discovery. In Venice, we wandered through the famous St. Mark's Square, marvelling at the intricate architecture and its busy yet spiritual atmosphere.  We ambled along the quiet canals, crossing the historic Bridge of Sighs, and indulged in the renowned Venetian experience of a gondola ride, serenaded by the romantic strains of 'O Sole Mio'.

Our visit to the Leaning Tower of Pisa left us in awe of its precarious lean, seemingly defying gravity with dramatic tilt.  Even though, feeling that it could fall over at any moment, this amazing landmark left a lasting impression on both Mam and me.

The tranquil evenings spent watching the sunset over the shimmering waters truly captured the essence of our Italian adventure. The gentle ripple of the waves against the shore, the golden hues of the setting sun painting the sky in an array of colours. It was a scene straight out of a dream.

As Mam and I prepared for bed on our last night in Italy, her unexpected question pierced the air, leaving me numb with shock.

"Are you pregnant?" she asked, her words hanging heavy between us. I stood before her, rendered speechless by the sudden enquiry. How could she possibly know? I hadn't even confirmed it myself. Before I could think of a response, Mam continued, her words cutting through the silence.

"Have you had sex with Tony?" Her directness left me trembling, unable to find the words to express the truth. Tears welled up in my eyes, revealing the emotions I had been trying to hide. Though the heavy silence between us felt unending, I found the courage to break it.

"Mam, I'm so, so sorry," I whispered, my voice filled with remorse. "I don't know what to do or say. I know I've let you down." My confession was marked by the pressure of guilt that burdened me. But within the despair, a flicker of hope emerged.

"But you never know," I continued, my voice tinged with uncertainty.  "I might still come on tomorrow."  It was a feeble attempt to cling to the possibility that my fears were unfounded, that the nightmare I found myself in might turn out to be just a bad dream.  I braced myself for Mam's response, unsure of what to expect.  Would she offer words of comfort or further reproach?  In that moment of vulnerability, all I could do was wait, hoping against hope for a glimmer of understanding through the pain and disappointment that engulfed us both.  After what seemed like an eternity, I finally found the courage to speak.

"How did you know?" I asked.  Mam replied by saying that she could see changes in my breasts that were very evident when I wore the see-through white negligee she had bought me for my holiday!

Mam's expression was a mixture of sadness and anger, her emotions swirling in a turbulent storm. Though she had had her suspicions, it seemed as though the reality of the situation was too much for her to bear. Her disappointment hung heavy in the air, visible and suffocating.  I felt her eyes staring at me, and it was as though she couldn't understand how I could have made such a massive mistake.  As I looked into her eyes, I couldn't help but wonder what thoughts raced through her mind.  Was it because she knew all too well the pain and challenges that lay ahead?  Or perhaps she couldn't bear to see me follow in her footsteps, making the same mistakes she had made in her youth.  The questions swirled in my head but I had no answers to offer.

All I knew in that moment was that we needed to go to bed and try to find relief in sleep.  As I lay there, tears streaming down my cheeks, the sound of my own sobs merging with Mam's cries echoed in the silence.  It was a stark reminder of the vulnerability we both shared, the rawness of our emotions evident for each other to witness.

In that moment of shared anguish, I couldn't help but reflect on the parallels between this moment and my childhood, when I would hear Mam cry into her pillow late at night.  How could I have brought this pain upon her, knowing first-hand the agony of watching a loved one suffer?  The weight of my actions laid heavy, suffocating me with guilt and remorse.

As I drifted off into a fitful sleep, haunted by the echoes of our shared sorrow, I vowed to do whatever it took to make things right, to mend the fractured pieces of our relationship and restore the trust that had been shattered by my indiscretion.  But for now, all I could do was seek some form of light in the darkness and pray for a glimmer of hope to guide us through the storm.

The journey back to England unfolded with a conversation between Mam and I about what lay ahead.

The weight of uncertainty cast a shadow over any shared silence.  My future now lay in the hands of the man I loved, but doubts gnawed at the edges of my mind.  Did he love me enough to support me in the months ahead?  As we discussed the choices before me, I couldn't help but notice a shift in Mam's perception of me.  The disappointment, sorrow, and anger she felt were obvious, etched into the lines of her tired face.  I understood her feelings all too well, recognising the pain and betrayal I had caused.

A beginning of understanding began to blossom between us despite our troubled emotions.  In the shared vulnerability of our conversation, I felt relief in knowing that Mam would stand by me, no matter what choices I made.

As Mam and I embarked on the last part of our journey, she gently reminded me of the urgent need to speak with Tony and confront the decisions that lay ahead.  Depending on the choices I made, we would have to consider whether to disclose the situation to Auntie Glenis, Uncle John, and other close family members who had been a part of my life since birth.

The gravity of the situation became more stressful as Mam continued to outline the potential demands I might face.  One looming issue was the lingering hostility toward Italians, stemming from the effects of the war.  Even though two decades had passed since the end of the war, the scars of conflict still lingered.  How would our families and communities react if Tony and I decided to get married?  As the miles passed, so did the multitude of questions swirling in my head, each one adding to the turbulence of our journey.  How would Tony react to the news?  What would our families say?  Would our love be strong enough to weather the storms that lay ahead?

# Twenty-nine

*O*n arriving home I knew I had to talk to Tony as soon as possible.  Little did he know, but his life was about to undergo a massive change.  After a night of broken rest in my own bed, I woke early with one thing on my mind: to confront Tony.  Mounting my bike, I pedalled swiftly to his home on St. Peter's Road where he resided with his sister and brother-in-law.

He was surprised by my early visit but welcomed me inside, his expression concerned as he sensed something was wrong.  We were supposed to meet later that day but I couldn't wait.  I asked if we could take a walk, explaining there was something urgent I needed to discuss.  He immediately agreed and we set off towards the nearby park in Spinney Hill.

We found a bench near the bandstand.  I composed myself and without hesitation, revealed the news: I was pregnant.  The colour drained from Tony's face, shock rendering him momentarily speechless.  I yearned for reassurance, for him to hold me close and promise everything would be okay.  But instead, his response was practical, almost detached:

"What are we going to do?"

His uncertainty cast a shadow over our once bright dreams.  Mam had always been my pillar of support, assuring me that marriage wasn't a necessity, that we could manage just fine, as she had done.  But my desire to marry and start a family burned fiercely within.

Tony's hesitation came from a different source.  He was torn between his love for me and the weight of familial expectations back in Italy.  His parents held traditional views, and this sudden twist in our plans was far from what they had envisaged for their son.

I grappled with the discord between my desires and the practicalities of our situation.  Was it fair to ask Tony to choose between his love for me and his family's approval?  Conversations turned into debates, emotions running high as we tried to achieve the delicate balance between love and duty.  Despite the uncertainty, one thing remained clear.  Our love was real, our relationship unbreakable.  As days turned into weeks, the pressure mounted.  The weight of expectations bore down on us, threatening to tear us apart.  Would we buckle under the pressures of society and family, or would we forge our own path, hand in hand, unyielding in our love?

For the next two weeks, Tony and I found ourselves wrapped in deep discussions about our future together. During these conversations, I made my position clear to him.  I didn't want him to feel compelled to marry me just because I was pregnant.  I firmly believed that pregnancy shouldn't be the sole reason for marriage.

Nothing was certain.  I eventually decided that, regardless of Tony's or anyone else's opinions, I was going to keep the baby.  This decision was mine to make, and I was determined to stand by it, no matter what!

Tony knocked on the front door and, as I opened it, I could feel the tension in the air.  We escaped to the comfort of the front room, where Tony's expression seemed to convey a mix of nerves and determination.  It was there, in everyday surroundings, that he poured his heart out.

In a heartfelt confession, he expressed his love for me and his sincere hope to marry me, not just for the sake of our forthcoming child, but for the genuine love and commitment he felt towards me.  His words filled the room with a warmth that I hadn't felt in a long time, but I couldn't shake the size of the demands that lay ahead.

We contemplated the future and saw an intimidating task before us. How and when were we going to break the news to Auntie Glenis?  Her traditional values and unwavering loyalty to old-fashioned ideals made telling her a daunting prospect.  The thought of alarming and disappointing her with news of my pregnancy at 18, coupled with having an Italian boyfriend, something she might view with disapproval, sent shivers down my spine.  I could almost hear Auntie Glenis's distain echoing in my head, chastising me for causing Mam such distress and defying social norms.  The fear of her judgment made me feel utterly irresponsible, and the prospect of facing her seemed like having to navigate a minefield of expectations and acceptable behaviour.

Tony and I made our way into the living room where Mam was engrossed in a television programme.  We nervously sat down beside her, the weight of our announcement heavy on our minds.  Taking a deep breath, we shared our decision: we were going to get married.  True to her supportive nature, Mam responded with a warmth that instantly eased our nerves.  She showered us with her best wishes and sincere congratulations, her encouragement and support were tireless during these very worrying times.

But as the initial wave of excitement settled, Mam's practical nature kicked in.  She calmly outlined the next steps we needed to take.

"First things first," she began, "we need to inform the family, including Auntie Glenis.  And you'll need to let your workplace know about the pregnancy."

Her words, spoken with a sense of urgency and responsibility, brought home the reality of our situation.

Amid the whirlwind of preparations, Mam gently reminded us,

"Decide on the wedding venue first," she advised, "and remember, the wedding banns will need to be read out for the next three Sundays."

Although Mam was busying herself planning for the future, I was overwhelmed by the sudden flow of decisions and responsibilities. The prospect of dealing with this new world of marriage and parenthood seemed daunting, and I realised that I had much to learn about what lay ahead.

The following six weeks were a whirlwind of activity, to say the least. Through the fuss of preparations for the upcoming wedding, Mam was my pillar of strength. Her constant reassurance, her support and tireless assistance became the rock upon which I leaned during this hectic time. The countdown to my wedding day grew closer. I couldn't help but marvel at the support that surrounded me. Friends, family, and even distant relatives rallied behind me, offering their assistance in countless ways. Their generosity, both emotional and financial, made the seemingly impossible task of planning a wedding suddenly possible.

At last, Tony and I stood hand in hand on our wedding day, surrounded by the warmth and love of our closest friends and family. It felt as though we had been transported away from the trials and uncertainties of our past.  The date and place are clear in my memory; September 1965, St Peter's Church in Leicester.

The prospect of marriage and motherhood had seemed like distant dreams, overshadowed by fear and uncertainty.  Yet, here we were, on this beautiful autumnal day, taking our vows and beginning a new chapter together as husband and wife.

Mam stood radiant, taking her place in the front pew of the church, pride beaming from her eyes as she supported my frail Grandad who greeted me with a tender smile.  Seeing Mam and Grandad side by side made my day extra special.

With the wedding formalities now over, Tony and I walked back down the aisle as a married couple.  The sight of Miss Jane, standing at the back of the church, truly took my breath away.  Her unexpected presence filled me with so much happiness.  My former Sunday School teacher and mentor had played an important role in shaping my early life, instilling in me the courage and fortitude to steer me through its demands.

It was almost unreal how seamlessly my life changed after Tony moved into Crafton Street, the addition of his presence effortlessly fitting into the spaces in our home.  It made perfect sense for him to join us; there was ample room to accommodate us as man and wife, even with the coming of a new addition to the family.

My due date drew nearer. I couldn't help but think about the implications of the impending arrival. Unlike my own birth, my baby's birth was to take place in hospital but on discharge I would be welcoming my first child into the very same home where I had taken my first breath 18 years earlier.

My thoughts drifted to Mam, the basis of my existence, whose boundless love and support had been my guiding light through every twist and turn of life. I realised the inadequacy of words to express the magnitude of my emotions. How could I ever convey the depth of my love for the woman who had given me everything, life, happiness, and a sense of belonging?

The initial weeks of marriage passed and an unhappy realisation settled over me like a heavy fog. Despite the vows exchanged and the promises made, I couldn't stop the unsettling feeling that I had made a grave error, a mistake that would cast the darkest of shadows over me. Mam's words echoed in my mind:

"You made your bed, now you must lie in it." I couldn't help but acknowledge the bitter truth her words held. With a keen insight into the situation, Mam didn't miss a thing. She understood all too well the control that Tony was exerting over me, the invisible chains that bound me to his intent.  Despite the mask I wore to shield her from the pain I endured, she saw through it, recognising the hurt that lay hidden beneath my forced smiles.  For her sake, I tried to hide my sorrow beneath a layer of false happiness, masking the wounds inflicted by Tony's actions.

Behind closed doors, the façade crumbled, leaving me to bear the brunt of his cruelty in silence.  I was in despair, clinging to a fragile hope that perhaps, with the arrival of our baby, Tony would undergo a miraculous transformation.  I longed for him to shed the layers of control and indifference, jealousy and insecurity, and to embrace the role of a loving husband and father with open arms.

There was one source of support in the midst of all this: Mam.  Despite the restrictions imposed by Tony, which limited my interactions with anyone outside our home, she remained constant, offering peace and comfort when I needed it most.  She was the one person I could turn to, the one companion I could confide in and spend time with.  Together, we found pleasure in simple outings to the shops, where we eagerly set about preparing for the arrival of the baby, examining the aisles, carefully selecting items for the baby's layette.  In those days, it was impossible to know what we were expecting so we opted for timeless colours, soft whites and gentle lemons that would be suitable regardless of whether we welcomed a little boy or a little girl into our lives.

Tony arrived home after his shift at Hillcrest Hospital one afternoon with news that shook our household.  Grandad wasn't doing too well.  Grandad seemed confused, agitated, and was battling with a persistent chesty cough.  This news was obviously concerning so Mam and I decided to pay him a visit at the hospital that very evening.  There was a silent heaviness in the air in the familiar corridors and a sense of dread that hung over us.

Grandad was nowhere to be found in the day room where he typically spent his time.  With a sinking feeling in the pit of our stomachs, we made our way to his ward.  The sight that greeted us was a stark contrast to our previous visit just a few days before.  Grandad was lying in the hospital bed, a mere shadow of his former self.  His once lively eyes were now dull and lethargic, and the lines of worry, etched deep into his wrinkled forehead, spoke volumes of his suffering.  We approached the nurse in charge for information.  She gently informed us that Grandad was struggling with a severe chest infection and was undergoing treatment with antibiotics, fluids, and rest.

Mam's voice broke the solemn silence, her words heavy with sorrow as she spoke of Grandad's profound grief over the loss of his beloved wife, Martha.  It was as though a piece of him had died with her, leaving behind a hollow emptiness that he struggled to fill.

The following day, as Tony departed for work, the house was quiet and solemn. Tony promised to be by Grandad's side as much as possible and to keep both Mam's workplace and mine informed should Grandad's condition take a turn for the worse. With his reassurances, we set off for work that day, confident that Grandad would soon recover.

However, tragedy struck with devastating haste. On that fateful afternoon, as the sun cast long shadows across the room, Grandad died. The news hit us like a sledgehammer, shattering us with shock and disbelief in an instant. Through the crushing grief, there was a small comfort; Tony had been with Grandad in his final moments, offering him care and friendship in his time of need.

Though our hearts were heavy with sorrow, there was a sense of closure in knowing that Grandad had found peace in the arms of his beloved Martha. However, in the midst of our distress, the question that was continually on my mind was: how much more could Mam take?

In the quiet moments of reflection, I knew that Nana and Grandad were watching over us, their spirits guiding us through the darkness.  Their legacy lived on in our hearts, a sign of hope in the midst of our sorrow.

# Thirty

*I*t is the way of the world that when one door closes, another one opens.  This sentiment couldn't have been truer for my family, especially with the arrival of our first child, Paul, born in 1966.  His entrance into the world marked a new chapter, just nine weeks after the passing of his great grandad.

Gazing at my new-born son in his cot was a surreal experience.  The tiny bundle of perfection sleeping before me just seemed too incredible to be real.  It was as though I was dreaming, but his gentle breaths reassured me that this moment was, indeed, reality.  Every tiny feature, from his delicate fingers to his button nose, filled my heart with overwhelming love and wonderment.

Time seemed to stand still in that quiet room as I marvelled at the miracle before me, bathed in the soft glow of the night light.  I knew I would treasure this moment forever, the beginning of a journey filled with boundless love and endless joy.

Tony was about to experience a revelation unlike any other.  As was customary back then, he was only informed of Paul's arrival when he rang the hospital the following morning and then had to wait until visiting time at 2pm before he could see his son for the first time.

As visiting time arrived, I could hardly contain my excitement.  I spotted Tony walking through the ward doors, a huge bunch of flowers in his arms.  By now, I was waving frantically, eager for him to see where I was.  He finally spotted me and hurried over, a wide smile spreading across his face.

He arrived at my bedside, leaned over and kissed me.  Then he turned his attention to the bundle in my arms.  Our new-born son, Paul, was cradled gently, his tiny features soft and delicate.  Tony just stood there, looking in amazement, his eyes wide and filled with emotion.  He reached out and carefully held Paul´s tiny hand, utterly fascinated by his delicate fingers.

Tony stayed with us for the entire visiting time.  The love and pride he felt for his new son were overwhelming.  We spent those precious moments together as a new family, captivated by the perfection of our little miracle.

Meanwhile, Mam shared in our joy, ecstatic at the arrival of her grandchild.  She made a special trip to the local baby shop on Wharf Street where she carefully selected Paul's first outfit: a beautiful pale blue romper suit made of silky material, incorporating delicate white and blue smocking.  It was a sign of the love surrounding Paul's arrival, a symbol of new beginnings and cherished moments to come.

I spent the usual 10 days in the hospital following Paul's birth before I was finally allowed to return home. However, stepping into the familiarity of home was just the beginning.  Reality struck hard as I realised the responsibilities awaiting me as a new mother.  This should have been a time for Mam to take a step back, to relax and enjoy her role as a grandmother.  Instead, she was burdened with the task of helping her 18-year-old daughter care for her new-born son.  Mam never complained.  Instead, she was overjoyed and full of pride at the arrival of her new grandson, eagerly looking forward to the chance to show him off to the world.

The hospital staff had advised me to stay indoors with Paul for the first two weeks at home, taking in the precious moments of bonding and adjustment.  So, when the 14th day finally arrived, I was ready for a change of scenery.  It was time to venture out with my beautiful son.  Proud and excited, I placed Paul in his brand-new pram with a quilt and pillowcase in matching white and navy and a navy canopy to protect his eyes from the sun. As Mam and I strolled through the streets, I felt a sense of accomplishment, knowing that I had entered the world of motherhood with the dedicated support of my own mother by my side.

As the weeks passed, my life seemed incredibly bittersweet.  I was overflowing with love and pride for my son, Paul, and equally proud of the support and love provided by his Nana.  Without her, I felt like I would be nothing, and that realisation only grew stronger with each passing day.  Even in those early years of marriage, my husband's control over me was suffocating.  His jealousy consumed every aspect of my life, dictating my every move.  In his eyes, I was expected not only to raise our son but also to work, to maintain and manage the house, to cook, and to fulfil every expectation of a dutiful Italian wife.

Tony insisted that our children would be raised as Catholics and, therefore, we had to be married in the eyes of the Catholic Church.  I agreed because, naively, I thought Catholicism was the stronger faith, but I also went along with it to prevent more disagreements.  Despite Tony's attempts to persuade me to change my own religion, I firmly refused.  However, I had no choice other than to agree to take part in the six compulsory, two-hour teaching sessions, to learn about the faith and my duties as a wife and mother.

The one thing I did insist upon was that the sessions wouldn't begin until after our baby was born and life had settled down again.  I agreed to start my lessons in June 1966, and our Catholic wedding was set for September 1966, exactly a year after our first wedding.

As the date approached, I reflected on the journey that had brought us here and, although I didn't feel it necessary, nor wanted to marry again, I knew I had little choice.  I felt the event was sheer hypocrisy.  The only time Tony ever practised his faith was when he insisted we did not eat meat on Good Friday or when he demanded we all attend Midnight Mass on Christmas Eve!

The lessons were both challenging and enlightening, providing me with a deeper understanding of the Catholic faith.  I began to appreciate the reasons for the faith's traditions and customs.  Although I held onto my own beliefs, I was willing to recognise the differences between the two religions.

This second wedding could never be compared to our first.  I wore the same suit, but the similarities ended there.  I had no flowers, nor any trimmings.  I didn't even have my hair done.  Mam didn´t want anything to do with the occasion for various reasons.  She preferred to stay at home to look after Paul while Tony and I attended the church.  We were joined by Tony´s sister and her husband who served as our witnesses.  The service was conducted in Italian by an Italian priest, and I responded when needed as well as I could considering that I spoke no Italian.  After the service, the four of us went to a nearby café and celebrated with a coffee and a piece of fruitcake.

And so it was.  Amen to that!

I wanted more independence and fulfilment but found myself trapped in a world of emotional abuse.  It was a suffocating existence, one where my dreams and aspirations were overshadowed by the demands and expectations placed upon me by Tony's own uneducated ignorance.  Mam seemed content with the joy brought by her grandson but I couldn't shake the feeling that she deserved more.  I was unable to break free from the chains of my marriage, bound not only by a sense of duty and obligation, but also by fear.  Each day became a struggle to balance the demands of my husband with the desire to provide a better life for myself and my son.  I clung to the hope that one day I would find the strength to break free from the emotional prison in which I found myself trapped.  Sadly, it took me 36 years to leave him.

Tony's new job at the local shoe factory, where he worked as an unskilled labourer, brought in minimal pay for maximum hours; making ends meet remained a constant struggle.  To alleviate the financial strain, I took on a job at the Twinlock Lingerie and Knitwear factory on Humberstone Road, working evening shifts from 6pm to 10pm.  This arrangement meant that Mam could care for Paul and prepare meals during my absence.

I agreed with her insistence that it was necessary to bring in additional income to support our growing family, yet I couldn't help but feel guilty about leaving Paul in her care.  Nevertheless, I pushed aside my concerns, knowing that every penny earned was crucial for our survival. In an attempt to repay her for her untiring dedication, I took on the responsibility of household chores during weekends, ensuring that she could enjoy some much-needed rest and relaxation. Whether it was simply taking Paul out for a stroll in Abbey Park, I wanted to make sure that Mam knew how much her sacrifices meant to me.

As the days turned into weeks and the weeks into months, the routine of balancing work, family, and financial struggles became the norm. Yet, among the challenges, the bond between Mam, Paul, and me grew stronger. In moments of quiet respite, surrounded by the simple joys of family, I had the strength to continue forging ahead with the determination to create a better future for us all.

Tony seemed indifferent to the depth of the relationship between me and Mam, or the special bond she shared with Paul. His priorities were clear: as long as he returned home to a wife who didn't complain, a tidy living room (despite the presence of a toddler), and a mother-in-law who didn't interfere in his life, he was content. His expectations bore down on me, further adding to the already immense pressure of juggling work, household responsibilities, and caring for our son. Regardless of my efforts to maintain peace and order in the household, Tony's satisfaction seemed elusive, his demands ever-present.  I couldn't help but feel frustration and resentment building up inside me.  The sacrifices I made, the effort I put into maintaining the façade of domestic bliss, all seemed to go unnoticed or unappreciated by him.

I cherished my job at Twinlock.  It was hard work, but it offered me a reprieve from the struggles of home life.  Conversations with my predominantly female co-workers ranged from men and relationships to nights out, husbands, boyfriends and children.  In those moments, my life didn't seem so bad.  But it was a world of pretence.

Behind the deception of a perfect life, I concealed the reality of my marriage, a relentless cycle of emotional and, tragically, physical abuse.  Despite the trust and friendship with my co-workers, I couldn't bring myself to confide in them about the turmoil I faced at home.  Shame and fear held me back from admitting the truth about my situation.  The thought of exposing the cracks in my seemingly perfect life filled me with dread. How could I possibly admit that the image I projected was far from reality?  So, I buried my pain beneath a pretence of smiles and laughter, making out that everything was fine when, in truth, it was anything but. The fear of judgment and stigma kept me silent and I remained trapped in a cycle of secrecy and suffering.

# Thirty-one

$S$ince the late 1950s and spanning over a decade, the
City Council had been implementing the Leicester Slum
Clearance order, raising compulsory purchase to address
housing issues.  While many residents from surrounding
streets, including Wharf Street and Russell Square, had
been relocated to various estates across the city such as
Braunstone Frith, New Parks, Eyres Monsell, and
Stocking Farm, some remained adamant in their refusal
to move to council estates, particularly to any of those on
offer.

Among the houses involved was ours, 12 Crafton
Street.  Mam and Grandad were adamant in their
decision not to leave their home for an alien estate.
However, time passed and our neighbourhood underwent
a transformation for the worse.  Houses stood as mere
shells, streets disappeared, and familiar faces vanished as
friends moved away.

With Grandad no longer in the picture, Mam was left
to handle the decision-making process alone.  I could
sense the heaviness in her heart as she faced the prospect
of leaving behind the house that had been her place of
safety and shelter for so long.  The thought of uprooting
from the place where Mam and I had built a lifetime of
memories felt unreal.  It wasn't merely about leaving

behind bricks and mortar; it was about bidding farewell to a precious chapter of our lives, to the well-known streets and neighbours who had become like family. We were saying goodbye to a way of life.

Mam and I faced a dilemma as we considered the properties being offered to us. On the one hand, we knew that accepting one of these properties would provide us with amenities like a bathroom and central heating. These were luxuries we wanted, especially for Paul's comfort and well-being. On the other hand, we couldn't ignore the fact that the areas where these properties were located were less than ideal, perhaps not the best environment in which to raise a child.

Ultimately, we made the difficult decision to prioritise Paul's future above all else. We knew that compromising on the neighbourhood we lived in could have long-lasting consequences for him. It wasn't an easy choice, but it was the right one for our family. We remained hopeful that the right opportunity would present itself, the chance of a place where we could have both the comforts we deserved and the ideal environment for raising Paul.

During this time of turmoil, Tony faced the unfortunate reality of losing his job again, adding even more pressure to our already strained situation. Desperate for a solution, Tony reached out to an acquaintance, Mr. Poli, who owned a fish and chip shop in Belgrave Gate.  Through Mr. Poli, an opportunity arose: Assunta, Mr. Poli's niece, was selling the goodwill of her fish and chip shop located in Wharf Street.  The sale included rented accommodation which, while lacking heating and bathroom facilities, offered plenty of bedrooms for our family, including for Mam.

This prospect was a lifeline for us, a chance to secure stability within the chaos of our circumstances.  The only hurdle we had to overcome was where to get £1000 to secure the purchase of the business.  With no other options, we turned to Auntie Glenis and Uncle John for help.  Despite their disdain for Tony, they agreed to lend us the money, recognising the dire situation we were in.

With the terms agreed upon, we took a leap of faith into the unknown.  It was a risky undertaking, but one we were willing to tackle in the hopes of securing a brighter future for our family.

My 21st birthday arrived.  Mam threw me a wonderful celebration that I'll always fondly remember. I was dressed in a beautiful turquoise satin dress with a broderie anglaise jacket that she had specially made for the occasion.  It was doubly exciting because I had a special announcement to share.

The venue was filled with friends and family, and I played the role of the doting wife, showering Tony with affection, despite the internal turmoil I suffered. Looking back, I can't quite understand why I felt the need to portray our relationship as perfect when, deep down, I knew it wasn't. Tony had the knack of being charming, especially during social gatherings. He enjoyed being liked and knew exactly how to achieve it. Everyone appeared to admire him, captivated by his looks and his charm. But behind closed doors, a different side of Tony emerged, one that I never disclosed to anyone except Mam. She was the only person I trusted with the truth, knowing she would never betray my confidence. Tony's control over me was something I kept hidden, a secret I securely locked away.

However, I loved Tony very much and there was a genuine joy in my heart when I revealed to our guests that we were expecting our second child. I felt an overwhelming sense of happiness and contentment in that moment, surrounded by the love and support of everyone. Even though there were difficulties in our marriage, the prospect of expanding our family filled me with renewed love and hope. I realised that, despite the complexities of our relationship, there were moments of genuine love and happiness that we shared.

In 1969, as my due date approached, anxiety crept in, overshadowing the anticipation of welcoming our baby. One concern loomed large: the strict hospital visiting hours that clashed with the opening hours of our

fish and chip shop, leaving me worried that my husband
and son wouldn't be able to visit me during my hospital
stay.  Determined to find a solution, we made the
decision to pay for a private room at the St. Francis
Nursing Home on London Road, Leicester.  This ensured
that Tony and Paul could visit me outside of regular
hospital hours.

My due date came and went without any signs of
labour and I grew increasingly anxious.

Ten days later, I sought advice from my GP who
instructed me to go to the hospital immediately.  With
Mam stepping in to care for Paul, Tony drove me to St.
Francis in the car we had recently purchased.  The next
24 hours were filled with warm baths and regular doses
of castor oil mixed into a glass of orange juice.  This
regimen was the clinic's non-invasive way of
encouraging labour to commence.

Finally, after hours of waiting and a long labour, I
gave birth to a beautiful baby girl named Gemma.  I held
her for the first time feeling that wonderful rush of
emotions, love, joy, and overwhelming gratitude.  All the
pain and discomfort faded away, replaced by
indescribable wonder and admiration.  Looking down at
her tiny face, I couldn't help but marvel at the miracle of
life.  Her delicate features, her tiny toes, and her soft cry
filled my heart with an indescribable warmth.  Tears of
joy streamed down my cheeks as I realised just how

blessed I was to have this precious little girl in my arms. I held her close and made a silent vow to cherish and protect her with every fibre of my being. She was a precious gift, a reminder of the boundless love and miracles that life had to offer. I gazed into her eyes and knew that my life would never be the same again for she had already stolen my heart in the most profound way imaginable.

In a heart-warming gesture, Mam presented me with a beautiful frilly pink dress and a knitted white cardigan for my new baby daughter. Holding my two precious children in my arms, I knew I was overwhelmingly lucky to have them both in my life.

I was discharged home with my new family after 10 days of wonderful care and sharing a lot of the time with Tony, Paul, Mam and of course, our new daughter, Gemma. The confinement, delivery and drugs came to £48/10s/6d. (today's equivalent of £1000!)

The next couple of years brought a whirlwind of activity and decision-making for our family. Our fish and chip shop business was thriving to the point where we needed to make a crucial choice: either hire additional staff to help manage the workload or consider selling the business altogether. With Paul about to start school at Taylor Street and Gemma ready for nursery, the pressure was on to make the right decision, especially given the looming threat of compulsory purchase still hanging over our heads.

I wrestled with the dilemma of balancing my responsibilities at the shop with the need to provide my children with the motherly love and care they deserved. It felt as though the demands of the business consumed most of my time, leaving me longing to be more available for my children.

When a serious offer was made for the business and goodwill, we saw an opportunity for change. Selling for £2000 meant that we could finally repay Auntie Glenis and Uncle John the remaining £500 that we still owed them, relieving the financial worry and pressure it brought us. Furthermore, we would still have £1500 left over, which allowed us to secure a deposit on our first home.

It was a monumental decision, one that would determine the course of our lives. We were taking another leap into the unknown, guided by hope and determination. Most importantly, Mam now had a secure home with us in the pretty village of Sileby. Though our new home may have been modest in size, it provided all of us with a security and independence we hadn't experienced before.

Mam had her own space in the house in Sileby. No longer constrained by the limitations of council estates, outside toilets, or the absence of running hot water and bathroom facilities, she could truly flourish in her new environment.  It had taken hard work to find the perfect home for our family, a place where we could finally put down roots and build a life filled with love and stability.

In August 1972, we officially made the move to our comfortable village home.  It came with a price tag of £4750 and a mortgage of £32 per month but, with careful planning and saving, we managed to gather the necessary deposit and furnish the house to our liking. With everything in place, we eagerly headed to the mortgage company to collect the keys, ready to embark on this exciting new chapter of our lives.

# Thirty-two

*L*ife in Sileby was a stark contrast to the noise and rush of city life in Leicester.  I immersed myself in a friendly community where neighbours were more like family, and simple pleasures like walking children to the school bus became daily rituals.  Our days were marked by casual conversations with other parents where we would exchange stories, share advice, and revel in the humour of village living.  It wasn't uncommon to drop by each other's houses for a cup of tea or coffee, forging friendships that, in some cases, would last a lifetime.

One person who quickly became a true friend was Joan, who lived on the opposite side of the road.  Our friendship blossomed effortlessly, supported by shared experiences and the common connection of motherhood.  Our children, who were all around the same age, became firm friends, and our homes became places of fun and laughter and the occasional childish squabble.

Joan was the only person apart from Mam I could trust and confide in, especially during my darkest moments.  She saw through the pretence of happiness and recognised the truth, that I was living a lie, and that Tony was at the root of the problem.

Once again out of work, Tony decided to venture into a new business, purchasing an ice cream van and subcontracting for Eric's Dairy Ice Cream in Leicester. True to form, he threw himself into the venture wholeheartedly, establishing a healthy ice-cream round and even investing in special events like local shows and festivals.

Challenges we faced as a family saw moments of triumph and support that helped bring us closer together. And through it all, I found satisfaction and strength in friends like Joan, who stood by me through thick and thin, offering a shoulder to lean on in times of need and always making sure I wore a smile on my face.

Joan and I, along with our children, eagerly awaited the annual Sileby Parade and Gala. It was a tradition we cherished, a time for our families to come together and showcase our creativity. Weeks before the parade, we would work together, crafting costumes with care and enthusiasm and, on several occasions, we would see the dawn break before we eventually went to bed.

The day of the parade finally arrived in the summer of 1973, and the air buzzed with excitement. Joan and I donned our costumes as the 'Fruit and Nut cases' with peanuts dangling from our straw hats. We transformed our children into characters featuring the Robinsons Golly, the Yellow Brick Road, the Jolly Green Giant, the Saturday Cat, and Alice in Wonderland. Each costume was a labour of love, reflecting our dedication to the event.

The parade made its way through the village streets, our family proudly marching alongside other participants. Spectators cheered and clapped, marvelling at the colourful displays. We enjoyed every moment, basking in the friendship of our community. Joan and I enthusiastically joined the festivities of the gala while Mam had kindly offered to look after Joan's youngest daughter, Sarah, my precious 9-month-old goddaughter.

Sarah's delighted coos and playful giggles added to the infectious energy of the gala. It was a heart-warming moment to witness her taking in the sights and sounds of the gala with such innocent fascination.

At the awards ceremony, we were thrilled to have won five of the eight prizes! It was a credit to our hard work and creativity, a well-earned reward for our efforts. The sun set and the festivities continued into the evening. We celebrated our wins with laughter and excitement. It was a moment to cherish, a memory etched in our hearts forever. As we bid farewell to another successful year, we looked forward to the next Sileby Parade and Gala, eager to continue our tradition of fun and togetherness.

Joan and I shared a special friendship that distance couldn't break. Although we both moved to new addresses over the years, we never lost touch.  Mam and I would often meet her at the local café, where we would catch up on our lives and talk about what our kids were up to.  I missed her terribly now that we were no longer neighbours.  Our relationship was more like that of sisters.  Our friendship was so solid that I felt I could just look through my lounge window and see her standing there.

In 1991, Joan was diagnosed with breast cancer.  Despite her strength and undeniable spirit, she passed away in January 1993, at just 49 years of age.  I loved her laughter but, most of all, her cherished friendship.  The loss of such a close friend left me devastated.  I felt so empty and alone but, with Mam by my side, I began to face my grief and rebuild my world.  Mam knew exactly what to say and how to say it.  She knew how to act, and she guided me through the stages of grief I found most difficult to deal with.

Mam's continued support helped me find a way to honour Joan's memory and cherish the beautiful moments we had shared.  Though Joan was gone, the warmth of her friendship remained.

Life in Sileby posed challenges for Mam at times.  As the family grew, it became increasingly apparent that our living arrangements were less than ideal.  The small box room that served as the children's bedroom was becoming cramped, and the need for more space was urgent, especially as Paul and Gemma would eventually need their own bedrooms.

The winter of 1974 welcomed the newest addition to our family: Dave, our second son. He was perfect. I was in love all over again and so thankful to Tony for giving me another beautiful child alongside Paul and Gemma. Dave's arrival brought both enormous pleasure and a renewed sense of urgency to our living situation. With three children, the need for a larger home became more pressing than ever.

Dave was born at the Leicester Royal Infirmary. The care and attention we had received from the hospital staff during our stay were nothing short of exceptional, leaving me deeply appreciative of their dedication and professionalism.

I had watched the nurses hurrying around, tending to the needs of new mothers and their babies and had a moment of inspiration. Deep within me, a long-held ambition began to resurface, the dream of becoming a nurse. I realised in that moment, surrounded by the atmosphere of the hospital ward, that if I were to return to work, there was no other path I would rather follow. The opportunity to care for others, to support new mothers through the process of childbirth, felt like a calling, a purpose that resonated deep within me. With Dave nestled against my chest, I made a silent vow to myself to pursue my dream of becoming a nurse, to channel my passion and dedication into a career that would allow me to make a difference in the lives of others.

We adjusted to life with a new baby but it was clear that our current home was no longer sufficient for our growing family.  It was a big challenge but a glimmer of hope arrived on the horizon.  It came about through a conversation Mam had with Wendy, her hairdresser. Wendy told her that a flat was becoming available for rent in Syston in the near future, sparking Mam's interest in the possibility of securing her own home.  Determined to explore this opportunity, she expressed her intentions to reach out to the Syston council to enquire about the possibility of renting the flat.

This was exciting news indeed and I was very happy for Mam.  The prospect of her having her own space was wonderful and I eagerly began to see how we could organise our lives to support each other and prosper together.

I was, however, fully aware that our finances would be affected.  With this in mind I took a proactive step towards fulfilling my dreams and securing financial stability by applying for a job at the Leicester Royal Infirmary Maternity Unit.  The position of Nursing Auxiliary for three nights a week, Friday, Saturday, and Sunday, seemed like an opportunity not only to contribute financially but also to pursue meaningful work in a field I was passionate about.

Now there was a new hurdle to get over.  It was becoming clear that to secure a more stable future, the need for me to learn to drive was a must.  But now, how do I convince Tony?

Though hesitant at first, Tony finally recognised the practicality of the suggestion.  Deep down, he knew that for our family to thrive and overcome the challenges we faced, certain sacrifices and adaptations were inevitable. Learning to drive was just one such adjustment, albeit a significant one.

Learning to drive was quite tricky, but I found encouragement in the support of Mam and the guidance of my dedicated driving instructor, Bill Batts.  His patience was remarkable, his persistence was admirable, giving me the confidence and determination to persevere and to succeed.  With each lesson, I gained a deeper understanding of the rules of the road and improved my driving skills, gradually building confidence behind the wheel.

Finally, after six months of effort and preparation, the day of my driving test arrived.  I sat behind the wheel and, guided by the instructions of the examiner, I remained focused and composed.  With each manoeuvre executed flawlessly, my confidence soared.  I delivered a performance that surpassed even my own expectations. It wasn't long before I received the news that I had passed my driving test on my very first attempt at the age of 31. It was a moment of triumph, proof of the power of perseverance and the determined support of those who believed in me.

The long-awaited day finally arrived when Mam moved into her own home, marking a momentous milestone of independence. The flat in the small town of Syston, situated on the second floor, welcomed her with its pristine cleanliness and tasteful decor, a place she could call her own.

I happily watched her settle into her new home, feeling fulfilled. It was evident that this was exactly what she wanted and deserved, a place where she could flourish and reclaim her identity. This moment was enormously significant so I made it my priority to ensure that her transition was as smooth as possible. From organising the logistics of the move to lending a helping hand with unpacking and arranging furniture, I spared no effort in supporting her through this important change.

This was more than just a change of address for Mam. She had weathered many storms in life, and now, she was finally reaping the rewards of her strength and perseverance. In the days and weeks that followed,

Mam's new home became a place of peace and quiet, a place where she could truly be herself.

Every Friday afternoon, as the week drew to a close, Mam would make her journey from her work in Leicester to Sileby, looking forward to the time she would spend with us over the weekend.  Throughout Saturday and Sunday, she was the backbone of our family, tending to the needs of the children, preparing meals, and ensuring that I had enough rest to face the demands of the night ahead.

On Monday mornings, as dawn broke and the city stirred awake, I would wearily make the journey home from work, then drive Mam to her workplace, ensuring she arrived on time to start her day.  While our arrangement was far from perfect, it was successful due to the strength of our commitment to one another.  The children gradually assumed more responsibility as they matured, easing the burden that lay on our shoulders.

Immersed in the comings and goings of the Labour Ward, I loved my job.  It was a job that gave me great satisfaction and filled me with a profound sense of fulfilment and purpose.  Each day brought new situations and triumphs but, above all, it offered me the chance to witness the miracle of birth first hand.  Despite the inevitable ups and downs of the job, the opportunity to support mothers through the miracle of childbirth was, a privilege I was deeply grateful for.

I understood the importance not only of providing medical care but also of offering emotional support to mothers during times of difficulty.  Whether it was dealing with complications during delivery or offering words of encouragement and reassurance, I was grateful for the opportunity to be there for those in need.  Nursing was more to me than a job, it was a vocation, a calling that resonated from the very heart of me.  I had never desired any other career; in the world of healthcare, I found my true purpose.

Despite the demanding nature of my work schedule, of three night shifts each weekend, I was confident that the routine allowed me to balance my professional responsibilities with my personal life.

# Thirty-three

*M*am was a character, full of life and fun.  Like everyone else, she had her traits and habits that we enjoyed, laughed at or laughed about.  For example, every Friday, straight after work, she would arrive in Sileby armed with her bag of goodies, which the kids fondly dubbed 'Friday sweets'.

Paul, Gemma and Dave, our trio of mischief-makers, would eagerly swarm around her as she pulled out the treasures from her bag.  Among them, three bars of chocolate stood out as desirable prizes.  Mam laid down the rules: they could devour them all in one go, save one for each day, or indulge on Sunday.  But under no circumstances were they allowed to touch their siblings' chocolate.

The boys, naturally, being the rascals that they were, always opted to wolf down their chocolates immediately, giggling mischievously as they did so.  Then came Sunday, the day of reckoning for Gemma, who, having diligently saved hers, would find herself in the spotlight as her brothers attempted to sweet-talk her into sharing.

But Gemma was no pushover; she knew the value of negotiation.  With a triumphant smile, she'd barter with her brothers, demanding a fair trade for her precious chocolate.  In the end, everyone emerged as winners, with smiles on their faces and chocolate on their lips.

Mam had a lifelong love affair with food in general, and her dining habits were as entertaining as they were endearing.  Whether we were out for a meal or enjoying a Sunday roast at home, Mam's quirks never failed to bring a smile to our faces.

Whenever we dined out, Mam had the peculiar habit of observing what the waiters were serving to other tables.  Even before her own meal arrived, she'd twist her neck to catch a glimpse of passing dishes, commenting with delight,

"Oh, that looks nice," or wistfully murmuring, "I wish I'd ordered that."  Her expectation of what was going to be on our plates also added an extra layer of excitement and fun to our dining experience.

At the Sunday dinner table, Mam's customs were equally distinctive.  She approached her plate with methodical precision, starting with the vegetables, then moving on to the potatoes, followed by the Yorkshire pudding, and any other accompaniments.  But here's the thing: she always saved her meat until last.  It was a quirk we'd grown accustomed to, part of the charm that made Mam who she was.

As she savoured each bite, Mam had another amusing habit that never failed to make us chuckle.

With impeccable timing, she'd watch us intently as we ate, and with every mouthful we took, she'd open her own mouth wide in solidarity, as if she were experiencing the flavours through us.

Mam's culinary escapades were a source of endless amusement for our family. Her love for food was not just about nourishment; it was a joyous celebration of life's simple pleasures. And in every meal shared together, we found laughter, love, and the unmistakable imprint of Mam's delightful personality.

Old habits indeed die hard and Mam's culinary traditions were no exception. Among her many thrifty practices, one stood out as a cherished family favourite: the art of collecting meat drippings. Whenever she cooked meat, whether it be a succulent roast or a hearty stew, Mam never let a single drop go to waste. As the meat sizzled in the oven or simmered on the stove, she'd carefully collect the precious drippings, pouring them into a container that seemed always to have a layer of previous drippings at the bottom. The fat would separate, leaving behind a golden pool of meat juices brimming with flavour.

This layer of liquid gold held a special appeal to Gemma and me. It was a treat unlike any other, a taste of home and tradition that we eagerly looked forward to. Mam's famous 'Dripping on Toast' became a favourite indulgence, a simple pleasure that brought us so much satisfaction.  In every dollop of dripping spread on toast, we tasted not just the rich flavour of the meat but also Mam's love and care woven into every meal.

Mam's knack for making the most of every morsel stemmed from her upbringing, a time when food was scarce and rationed.  She knew the value of stretching ingredients and transforming leftovers into new culinary delights.  Her resourcefulness was one of the qualities that defined her.  She may have been a product of a bygone era, but her culinary legacy lives on.

Mam was known for her unique relationship with food.  She had a way of savouring each bite, turning every meal into an event.  We often watched in amusement as she meticulously prepared her plate, taking her time to appreciate the colours, textures and aromas before she even took a taste.  She would then close her eyes and take a slow, deliberate bite, letting out a satisfied hum that signalled her approval.

This ritual of hers wasn´t just about eating; it was about experiencing food in its entirety.  She would talk about her meals with a passion that was almost an art form.  Her descriptions were vivid and detailed, making everyone around her yearn for a taste.

Mam´s granddaughter, Gemma, has inherited this gift for description.  Gemma was captivated by Mam´s cooking concoctions and habits and her tales about her culinary successes.  She would listen intently; her imagination painting pictures of the dishes Mam was describing.  As she grew older, Gemma found she had the same talent.  She can describe a meal so vividly that listeners can almost taste it themselves.  Her words are like brush strokes, creating a picture so detailed that the flavours seem to come alive.  You really don´t need a lot of imagination to be enticed by the aromas, the taste and the artistry of the meals she describes.

But Mam´s legacy didn´t stop there.  Two of her great-grandchildren, Jamie and Florence, have also inherited a love of food.  However, they have taken a more scientific approach, having chosen to study the variety of elements of food and nutrition.  Their knowledge of ingredients and properties of food and its preparation will assist them both in their future careers. They hope to help people make better food choices and to understand the importance of a balanced diet.  Their work is a blend of art and science, much like Mam´s own approach to food.  And so, Mam´s idiosyncrasies with food live on through generations who appreciate and celebrate the delights of the culinary world.

As Mam's life settled into a comfortable rhythm, she embraced a newfound sense of adventure, jetting off to explore the world.  It was lovely to see her finally indulging in the pleasures of travel, soaking in new sights and experiences.

Even in the excitement of her globe-trotting escapades, Mam remained firm in her selfless traditions, much to our delight and amusement.

Without fail, at each destination, Mam would diligently send two postcards back home. One would showcase the breath-taking scenery of her surroundings, a snapshot of the picturesque landscapes she encountered on her journey.  The other postcard however, always brought out a giggle or a blush, a saucy cartoon character pictured on the front, a playful nod to her mischievous spirit.

We eagerly awaited the arrival of these postcards, each one a tiny glimpse into Mam's adventures at home and abroad and a testament to her thoughtfulness.

But it didn't end there.  No indeed!  The pièce de résistance awaited us upon her return: the souvenirs. Like clockwork, Mam would present us with a fridge magnet and a tea towel, each bearing the name of the place she had visited.  These gifts were simple yet meaningful tokens of her travels, reminders of the places she had explored and the memories she had made.  Her gestures, though small, spoke volumes about her love and thoughtfulness.  She may have been a creature of habit, but her predictable charm only endeared her to us more.

When Tony and I moved into our new home in
Mountsorrel in 1987, one of the first pieces of furniture
we bought was a charming Welsh dresser.  Its rustic
appearance and ample display space begged to be filled
with delicate treasures.  And who better to assist in
starting my collection than Mam?  She proposed adding
a touch of elegance to our lovely new home by starting a
china collection for the dresser.  Excited by the prospect,
we decided to take a mother-daughter trip to Lewis's,
the well-known department store situated in
Humberstone Gate.

Lewis's basement floor was a must for china
enthusiasts, displaying an array of exquisite collections
that dazzled the eye.  We wandered through the aisles
filled with delicate teacups and ornate plates and I found
myself torn between the multiple options before me.
How could I possibly choose just one?  After what felt
like an eternity of deliberation, a particular collection
caught my eye: Brambly Hedge by Royal Doulton.  Its
whimsical illustrations and intricate detailing spoke
volumes, transporting me to a world of enchantment and
nostalgia.

Among the plates on display, one stood out: 'Old
Oak Palace.'  It depicted a majestic oak tree against a
backdrop of lush foliage with an air of timeless elegance.
Without hesitation, Mam graciously purchased it for me,

and with great care, we placed it on the centre shelf of
the Welsh dresser.

'Old Oak Palace' took its pride of place, marking the
beginning of a cherished collection that would grow with
each passing year.  Each piece would not only decorate
our home but also serve as a tangible reminder of the
relationship between Mam and me.

Over the span of ten years, Mam showered me with
a generous collection of Brambly Hedge china, each
piece an insight into the enchanting world of the mice
and their seasonal adventures.  From the cosy warmth of
their homes in Brambly Hedge, the mice welcomed us
into their lives through the intricate illustrations that
decorated plates, tea-sets, mugs, clocks, and an array of
other objects.

Each item in the collection whispered tales of
weddings, birthdays, new arrivals, and the joyous
festivities that filled the four seasons of the calendar.  In
the springtime, we witnessed the blooming romance of
the mice as they exchanged vows in delicate ceremonies
set within colourful floral displays.  Summer brought
with it the jubilant celebrations of birthdays, with cakes
decorated with sugar flowers and candles.  Autumn saw
the expectation of new arrivals, as the mice prepared
cosy nests for their little ones, while winter nights were
filled with the sparkle of parties and balls in the grand
hall.

As the collection grew, so too did the cast of characters, with little figurines of the beloved mice joining the display.  Each figurine captured the heart of the characters we had come to love through the tales of Brambly Hedge, from the mischievous Wilfred to the elegant Primrose.  With every new addition to the collection, Mam and I shared moments of delight, reminiscing about the stories that had captivated us for so long.  The Brambly Hedge collection became more than mere decorative pieces; they were cherished heirlooms, soaked in memories of shared laughter and cherished moments spent together.

As I trace my fingers along the delicate designs today, I can't help but smile at the memories they create. The laughter shared over cups of tea, the quiet moments spent admiring each new addition, the joy of discovering a hidden gem among the busy aisles of a department store; these are the moments that will forever hold a special place in my heart.

# Thirty-four

*E*ven before I was able to understand about life and its hurdles, I knew Mam always tried to do her best. She faced challenges with a quiet determination, whether it was the loss of loved ones, the hardships of making ends meet or the worries I gave her over the years. Her brothers, Ben and Edward, too, were made of the same strong fibre.

In 1952, Uncle Edward and Auntie Mary exchanged vows, uniting their lives in marriage. Shortly after, they bought a lovely, detached bungalow in Mary's home town of Syston. It was a perfect start to their life together, filled with hopes, dreams, and the promise of a bright future.

Despite their love and devotion for each other, Uncle Edward and Auntie Mary faced a daunting reality: the heart-breaking realisation that their dreams of starting a family might never come to fruition.

On medical advice, they were told that Uncle Edward's chest disease posed significant risks, not only to his own health but also to any potential children they might have. It was a bitter pill to swallow, knowing the joy of children might forever elude them. As they came to terms with the unfairness of it all, they found a way to cherish the blessings they did have. They poured their love into their home, creating a warm and welcoming haven for them both.

Uncle Edward and Auntie Mary refused to let their unfulfilled dreams define them. They grabbed each day, making the most of what life had to offer. Uncle Edward was more than just another family member; he was the father figure I never had. His visits, accompanied by Auntie Mary, were a highlight in our lives, especially when Nana was still with us.

Each visit followed a comforting routine. We'd gather around the table for tea, sharing stories and laughter as we caught up on each other's lives. Then came the games. Uncle Edward was always up for a round of our favourites, his playful competitiveness adding to the joy of the moment.

Their visits were special for other reasons too. It was the little things, like his willingness to help Mam with the evening chores. One of his regular tasks was to prepare the tin bath for my weekly soak. Before I stepped into it, they both wished us,

"Night, night, God Bless," and went home.

Sunday evening visits continued but now in Sileby. Just like when I was a child, my own children eagerly awaited their arrival, excited for the chance to spend time with their Uncle Edward and Auntie Mary. The routine remained familiar; tea, games, and laughter filling the air as we gathered around the table, creating new memories while reliving old ones.  Uncle Edward's playful spirit hadn't lessened with age and he delighted in sharing the same games with my children that he had played with me years ago.

His health, held together by his own courage and determination, began to worsen.  The love they had for each other and for our family only seemed to grow stronger with each passing day, a ray of hope in the darkness.

Then, in 1990, tragedy struck.  Uncle Edward's battle with illness came to an end, leaving behind a void that could never be filled.  He was just 59 years old, his life cut short far too soon.

Earlier that same year, our family holiday in Italy had seemed like a dream.  Laughter had danced in the air as we recounted the days adventures, the scent of tobacco leaves, the family's cash crop, still lingering on our clothes.  Rosa, Tony's mother, with her gentle smile and petite frame, had gone to bed early as she always did.

The following morning, Rosa's absence was immediately noticeable because she was usually pottering about from around 6am.  The house, once alive with her morning rituals, now stood silent.  Concerned, we rushed upstairs to her bedroom to find her still in bed but unconscious. Tony immediately picked her up and carried her to the car. She sat, leaning on me in the back of the car, not stirring at all.

It was a 50km. journey to the hospital in Benevento, but within ten minutes, I noticed Rosa had died in my arms. I asked Tony to stop the car then told him. It was a devastating experience for us both.

Rosa's journey had ended, her pain, gone. The one thing we could hold onto was that she didn't linger or suffer. In the tender embrace of family, we found comfort from the knowledge that she had found peace in her final moments.

As if the loss of Rosa and Edward weren't enough to test our family's toughness of spirit, fate dealt us yet another cruel blow in the May of the following year. They say misfortune comes in threes and, for our family, that expression proved painfully true as another tragedy struck, this time directed at Ben's family.

Ben was now married to his second wife, Anne, who gave birth to Michael in early 1970. Michael's siblings, Adam and Louise, arrived within the next three years. The children were similar in age to my own and they all got on very well, especially as teenagers. They always enjoyed each other's company at family occasions where they would sit around a table, behaving like typical teenagers and having fun.

One morning in late Spring 1991, Michael was getting ready for work at the Post Office headquarters in Leicester.  During breakfast, he complained of feeling unwell.  Just as he was about to explain how he felt to his mother, he collapsed, his head landing on the table with a heavy thud.

Anne immediately called for an ambulance and the crew wasted no time in getting Michael to the hospital. The initial concern was that Michael might have an infectious disease but the doctors ruled that out after several tests.  The negative results left everyone anxious and confused, wondering what could have caused Michael's sudden collapse.  Michael lay in the hospital bed, aware of his surroundings but unable to stay awake for very long.

Mam and I visited Michael the day after his admission to hospital.  He looked poorly and tired so we only stayed for a short time.  Before we left, Michael held his hand out to me and gave me a gentle smile.  I took his hand and he said quietly,

"I love you, Auntie Anna."  Controlling my emotions was so hard, but I gave him a gentle hug, squeezed his hand and told him I loved him too.  That was the last time Mam and I spoke to him.

Shortly after we left, Michael had a heart attack.  He was immediately taken to the Intensive Care Unit and placed on a ventilator. Despite the medical team's best efforts, Michael's condition did not improve. After two weeks of intensive care, the difficult decision was made to end his treatment. Michael passed away due to complications of glandular fever and organ failure. He was just 21 years old. His loss was devastating, leaving a void in our family that could never be filled.

Ben and Anne's lives were in pieces. They struggled to find meaning in a world without Michael. There were days when the grief was overwhelming. Anne would spend hours in Michael's room, surrounded by his belongings. They clung to each other for support yet the path to healing seemed impossibly long.

As a family, we joined together in grief, each of us displaying feelings of disbelief, anger and profound sorrow. We talked freely, sharing memories of Michael. We cried openly, not holding back the tears that seemed endless. Every day, the stronger among us held the weaker ones together, creating a support system built on love and understanding.

Ben and Anne never fully recovered from the loss of their son but, somehow, found a way to carry on. Their lives, though forever changed, were once again filled with purpose and hope. They had learned to live with the pain and to honour Michael's memory by embracing life and finding joy in the small moments. Through their strength, they taught us a valuable lesson: that even in the face of unimaginable loss, it is possible to find a way forward.

Though the pain of our collective grief threatened to overwhelm us at times, we refused to let it define us. Slowly but surely, we began to pick up the pieces of our shattered hearts, finding comfort in the shared precious moments that brought light to our darkest days.  And so, we learned to laugh again, not in spite of our sorrow, but because of it.

# Thirty-five

*I*t was a quiet Sunday evening just before Christmas in 1980.  The loud ring of the telephone pierced the calm of our house in Sileby.  I picked up the receiver in the hallway, unaware of the unexpected turn the night would take.

I did not recognise the deep voice that greeted me on the other end, enquiring about Mam.  Suspicion crept into my mind as I asked for more information, asking the caller's identity and purpose.  To my shock, the response sent shivers down my spine.  He identified himself as a private detective, hired with the sole mission of locating Mam.

I struggled to understand the implications of his words.  Why would someone hire a detective to find Mam?  With a sense of unease settling in my stomach, I informed him that I couldn't disclose any information at that moment, promising to provide an update if he called back later, at 8pm.

I was extremely curious to know what it was all about but apprehensive of what might be on the horizon, casting a haze over our normally settled home.  As the echoes of the mysterious phone call lingered in the air, my mind swirled with questions, each one more insistent than the last.  I turned to Mam.

"Who could it be, Mam?" I begged, my words tinged with a mixture of fear and longing. But Mam remained determined, her gaze steady as she dismissed the possibility of the caller being my father.

Her certainty only intensified the doubt within me. Why was she so sure it wasn't him? Was it simply wishful thinking on her part, a desperate attempt to shield herself from the painful truth? Or did she possess knowledge that she was unwilling to share? As far as I knew the only man she had had a relationship with was my father! Deep down, a part of me yearned for the caller to be my father. Despite the many years that I had spent without him, there lingered a flicker of hope within me, a longing for reconciliation and closure.

But as I searched Mam's eyes for reassurance, I realised that some secrets were buried too deep to be unearthed. And in that moment of uncertainty, I faced the painful realisation that the truth might forever remain shrouded in mystery, leaving me to wrestle with the ghosts of the past alone.

As the clock reached 8pm, signalling the promised return of the caller, tension hung heavy in the air. I watched as Mam approached the telephone, her movements deliberate as she prepared to confront the mystery head-on. I listened in with bated breath, straining to catch every word of the conversation that unfolded. My ears tuned in with acute focus, desperate for any hint or clue that might shed light on the mystery that had fallen upon us.

In a quiet voice, Mam exchanged words with the caller, her voice steady.  Though I struggled to hear the details of their discussion, the severity of the situation left me counting every minute.  There was determination in Mam's voice as she arranged for the caller to contact her once again, this time at 9pm.  With this, their conversation drew to a close.

My mind teemed with questions as I waited for the next chapter in this unfolding saga.

As Mam sank back into the cushions of the settee, her behaviour caught my attention immediately.  She seemed startled, her usual composure evidently shaken.

"Who was it, Mam?" I pressed gently, my voice tinged with worry.  I couldn't shake the suspicion that perhaps it was my father attempting to reconnect with her after all these years of absence.  But before I could even voice that thought, Mam's response cut through the air with a stern finality.

"No," she said firmly, her tone leaving no room for further enquiry.  "Why on earth would he want to contact us now?"  Her words dispelled the momentary hope that had sparked.  The finality in her voice told me that questioning further would yield no answers.  It was clear that Mam was keeping something from me, something important.  I watched her retreat into her thoughts.  I knew that it was only a matter of time before the truth revealed itself but, until then, I could do nothing but wait.

Within a few minutes, Mam seemed to gather her thoughts and decided to confide in me about the events of the evening.  With a sigh, she began to unravel the mystery that had left her so shaken.

"The man on the phone," she started, her voice tinged with worry, "was a private detective working for a man called William (Bill) Maltby who wants to get in touch." The name struck me as unfamiliar, and I raised my eyebrows in confusion.

"Bill Maltby? But Mam, Dad's name is Matthew, not Bill," I interrupted, trying to make sense of the situation.  Mam nodded, acknowledging my confusion, before continuing with her tale.

"When I was 17," she recounted, her gaze distant as she delved into the past, "I was in love with this man. Just before he went off to war, we got engaged."

Her words painted a picture of a bygone era, a time when uncertainty loomed over every aspect of life.

"It's something you used to do in those days," Mam explained softly, a hint of sadness lacing her words.  "You got engaged just in case you never returned home again.  It was something people who lost loved ones in the war held onto."

As Mam shared this piece of her past with me, I couldn't help but feel a twinge of empathy for the young woman she once was, faced with the harsh realities of war and loss.  And as the pieces of the puzzle began to fall into place, I realised that there was much more to this story than I had ever imagined.

What had happened next had left Mam deeply hurt and seething with anger.  As she recounted the events, it became clear just how deeply she had been hurt by Bill's actions.  Mam revealed that Bill had abruptly called off their engagement following a false report from a so-called 'friend' who had told him Mam was pregnant. The mere accusation had shattered her world.  Of course, Mam wasn't pregnant at all, but convincing a man clouded by false information was an insurmountable task.  It was a betrayal that cut deep, leaving scars that would linger for years to come.

This betrayal marked the first in a series of disappointments for her, a blow to her trust in men that would shape her future relationships.  The pain of being let down so profoundly left her reeling, her heart guarded against the possibility of further hurt.

I listened to Mam's story unfold and the weight of her pain was evident, a stark reminder of the fragility of trust and the devastation that follows betrayal. I couldn't help but feel a surge of protective anger, wishing I could shield her from the pain of the past.

Growing up, I had always been puzzled by Mam's reluctance to date and her guarded feelings towards men. She seemed to carry a weight of mistrust, and her famous saying, 'I wouldn't have a man if his balls hung in gold,' left me both amused and perplexed. As a child, I couldn't grasp the depth of her sentiment, but as I grew older, the pieces of the puzzle started to fall into place. Mam's past experiences, particularly her broken engagement with Bill, had left scars that ran deep. The betrayal she endured had instilled in her a profound scepticism towards men and their intentions.

It wasn't until later in life, after hearing her recount the pain of her past, that I truly understood the meaning behind her words. Mam wasn't simply dismissing men for the sake of it; she was protecting herself from the possibility of further heartache. Her reluctance to open herself up to romantic relationships wasn't a sign of weakness but rather a testament to her strength and need for self-preservation. Mam had weathered storms of disappointment and betrayal, emerging with her spirit intact but guarded.

Reflecting on her famous saying now, I realise that it wasn't just a witty remark but a reflection of her unshakable resolve never to settle for anything less than she deserved.  In her own way, Mam taught me the importance of self-respect and the power of standing firm in the face of hardship.

"So, what are you going to do, Mam?" I asked, my concern evident in my voice.

"What are you going to tell him when he rings?" Mam's response was measured, her tone reflecting a sense of resolve tinged with caution.  She explained that she would entertain his call briefly, just long enough to gather her bearings and assess the situation.  After that, she planned to decide whether or not to allow him to contact her at the flat.

As I listened to her words, I felt so proud of her. Despite the turmoil she had suffered, Mam remained steady and composed.  She refused to let Bill's reappearance disrupt her sense of control or dictate her actions.  I couldn't help but admire her strength and determination.  Mam had been hurt before, but she wasn't allowing herself to be hurt again.  She was taking charge of her own narrative, refusing to be a victim of circumstances beyond her control.

<h2 style="text-align:center">Thirty-six</h2>

*B*ill and Mam met on several occasions in the first few months of their re-acquaintance with their feelings for each other growing stronger by the day.  I found that a bitter pill to swallow.  If anyone was going to come between Mam and me, it was going to be my father!

I didn't like Bill.  I couldn't explain why, but the dislike was deeply rooted, as if it had always been there, waiting for the right moment to surface.  The first time Mam brought him to our house, he arrived with a bottle of wine, wearing a smile that seemed too forced.  I immediately felt he was trying to buy my acceptance, and I was determined that any acceptance would be on my terms.  I would not be bought!

He was charming in a way that felt rehearsed, his compliments to Mam too sugary sweet, his laughter just a little too loud.  I watched him carefully, scrutinising every gesture and word, convinced that beneath his friendly exterior lay something insincere.  Mam seemed happier than I had seen her in a long time, but even that couldn't soften my attitude.  I tried to accept him, I really did.  But, in my eyes, he couldn't do anything right!

But what had Bill's past life got to do with me?  I still felt I needed to understand so I continued to question.  Why had Bill searched for Mam within a year of his wife's death from cancer?  What would his family think, and how would they respond to a new lady in their father's life?  My most important question was, given that he had done it once before, would he break Mam's heart again?

My resistance towards Bill grew stronger as the weeks passed.  His efforts to connect with me, his attempts to discuss my interests felt like strategies, not genuine gestures.  His closeness and tactile behaviour were certainly not welcome.  My husband Tony would soon have something to say if, without question, I responded acceptingly to Bill′s over-friendly behaviour.  He would have made my life unbearable if he had felt I was encouraging Bill or allowing him to be familiar with me.  Despite me asking Mam to tell Bill about Tony's jealous and abusive behaviour and not to show any familiarity towards me, Bill continued to anger Tony on several occasions just by being himself!

I realise now how wrong I was.

Bill wasn't trying to buy my acceptance; he was just trying to be part of our lives, to make Mam happy.  My selfishness blinded me to the simple truth; he was a good man who cared for Mam and wanted to care for me too.  My refusal to see past my own insecurities and preconceived notions hurt everyone, especially Mam.  It took years for me to understand that my dislike for Bill was never really about him.  It was about my fear of change, of someone new stepping into a place that had been just mine and Mam's. And of course, my husband made sure I never displayed any feelings towards Bill other than dislike!

While I knew deep down that Mam deserved happiness, companionship, and financial security, I couldn't shake off the twinge of jealousy and fear that gnawed at me. However, Mam made it clear that I couldn't interfere with her new-found happiness. I either had to accept it or remove myself from the situation, so remove myself I did.

The first few months were the hardest. The emptiness in my life, the absence of Mam's comforting presence, was almost unbearable. I missed our nightly chats on the phone, our shared laughter, and the simple companionship we had always enjoyed. Seeing her happy with Bill should have been enough for me, but the jealousy and insecurity were like a poison, clouding my judgment and my support for her. I would often take myself to sit in the cafe we used to frequent on a regular basis, hoping I would see her. I would pick up the phone willing myself to ring her number, but my stubbornness and feelings of hurt prevented me from doing so.

One day, a wedding invitation from Mam and Bill arrived, serving as a severe reminder of what was at stake. It was a moment of reckoning, a realisation that if I didn't mature and reconcile, I risked losing the person I loved most in this world.  With a heavy heart but determined to resolve the situation, I accepted the invitation.

I reached out, a tentative step, but one that Mam welcomed with open arms.  Our reunion was bittersweet, filled with apologies and tears.  Bill was there too, offering his own quiet understanding.  He and I talked, really talked, for the first time.  I learned about his past, his love for Mam, and his desire to be part of our family.

Time has a way of offering understanding.  From a distance, I could see the changes in Mam more clearly.  Bill's influence was undeniable; he brought a light back into her life that I hadn't seen in years.  She laughed more, smiled more, and seemed genuinely content.  And slowly, I began to realise that Bill wasn't replacing me in her heart, he was simply adding more love to it.

Rebuilding my relationship with Mam was an ongoing process, but a joyful one.  We started to create new memories together, blending our lives in a way that was worthy of the past while embracing the future.  Bill and I found common ground until, over time, he became someone I could trust.

I truly regret the time I lost, the moments I missed.  But I also understand that those months of separation were necessary for me to change and to see things from a different perspective.  Bill was never the enemy; he was the person who brought light and happiness back into Mam's life.

The wedding day arrived.  I stood witness to Mam and Bill's union, feeling thankful that I was there.  There was joy in seeing Mam radiant with happiness, yet a pang of regret lingered for the time lost in our rift.

Mam, now 63 years old, exchanged vows with Bill at Leicester Registry Office in June 1987.  The sincerity of the occasion served as a touching reminder of the endurance of love and the power of forgiveness.  As Mam and Bill embarked on this new chapter of their lives together, I made a silent vow of my own: to cherish every moment with Mam, to learn from the mistakes of the past, and never to take her love for granted again.

1987 marked a significant turning point in many aspects of our lives.  For Mam, it was the year she married Bill, marking the beginning of a new chapter filled with love and companionship.  Paul, too, found happiness as he began his own journey into married life.  Meanwhile, Tony and I reached a major milestone by purchasing our new home in Mountsorrel.  It was a symbol of stability and a place where we could build our future together.

On a personal note, I achieved a long-awaited goal by passing my entrance exam to start my nurse training.  After 15 years of dedicated service as a nursing auxiliary, it was finally my time to step into a new role and pursue my passion for nursing.  With Paul, Gemma and Dave all now more or less self-sufficient, I had the opportunity to focus on myself for a change.  It was a chance to invest in my own growth and fulfilment, something I had long put on hold while caring for others.

But perhaps most significantly, I was driven by a deep desire to make Mam proud.  Her support and sacrifices had paved the way for my success and I was determined to honour her by achieving my dreams.

I forged ahead in my nursing career.  In 1990, I achieved my dream of becoming a Registered General Nurse.  My first role took me to Ward 11, the Paediatric Ward at Leicester Royal Infirmary where I dedicated myself to caring for young patients and their families.

Just two years later, I was back in the classroom, studying tirelessly to qualify as a Cardiothoracic Nurse at Groby Road Hospital.  This new specialisation opened doors for me, leading me to transfer to a brand-new Glenfield General Hospital where I eventually rose to the esteemed position of Primary Nurse.  The long nights spent on duty didn't deter me; instead, they encouraged my ambition.  However, apart from my training years, by 2004 I had spent 25 years working the night shifts, and now older and feeling tired, I decided I needed a change.

I began a new venture, this time as a teacher, determined to impart my knowledge and experience to future generations of student nurses.  It was a role that filled me with purpose and pride, knowing that I was shaping the next wave of healthcare professionals.  It also gave me the opportunity to work through the day.

As I continued to enjoy further success and to achieve my goals, I was drawn to further education.  I pursued higher qualifications in management and teaching, eventually landing the role as a teacher/trainer in the subject of Safe Administration of Medicines.

With each achievement, I secured not only my future, but also the respect of my peers and colleagues. Above all else, I had the greatest satisfaction in knowing that I had made Mam proud.  Her encouragement had been the driving force behind my success.  I had achieved more than I had ever thought possible, but it was the pride in Mam's eyes that truly filled my heart, knowing that I had fulfilled her hopes and dreams for me.

## Thirty-seven

*W*ith the weight of exhaustion still heavy upon me from a night duty shift, I stumbled towards the front door, roused by the insistent ringing of the doorbell.  I was greeted by a sight that stopped me in my tracks: Mam and Bill stood on the doorstep, their expressions grave and troubled.  Even before they stepped inside, Mam's words pierced the air like a dagger to the heart.

"What do you know about Leukaemia?" she asked, her voice trembling with emotion.

In an instant, our worlds changed and would never be the same again.  The mere mention of the word sent a chill down my spine, filling the air with an over-whelming sense of dread and despair.

Leukaemia.  The word hung heavy between us, a stark reminder of the fragility of life and the cruel twists of fate that could tear loved ones apart in an instant.

We stepped inside and gathered around the kitchen table where Mam and Bill shared the devastating news: Mam had been diagnosed with Leukaemia.  Time seemed to stand still as we grappled with the magnitude of the news.  Tears flowed freely, merged with a sense of disbelief and helplessness that threatened to consume us all.

The following months were a whirlwind of trauma and uncertainty as Mam underwent numerous medical procedures.  Biopsies, draining of fluid and blood transfusions became routine as she battled against the relentless grip of the disease.  Despite the hardships, her spirit shone through.  With each passing day, she grew stronger, her determination to overcome the illness unshaken.  Slowly, over the course of two years, there came some hope.  The doctors delivered a cautiously optimistic prognosis: as long as Mam remained diligent with her medication and attended regular check-ups, she had a good many years ahead of her to enjoy life.

The blanket of uncertainty that had hung over us lifted, replaced by a profound sense of relief and gratitude.  At last, Mam was given the chance to reclaim her life, to embrace each day with renewed vigour and purpose.  It was a second chance at life, a reprieve from the shadow of illness that had loomed over her for so long.  It was a lantern of hope that illuminated the path forward, reminding us never to take life for granted.

Mam found comfort in watching television while she was regaining her strength.  Her favourite programme during this time was 'Take the High Road,' a Scottish TV soap filmed in the picturesque village of Luss, bordering the shores of Loch Lomond.  The show took her to a place of serenity and beauty and Luss was eagerly placed on her 'hit list' as a place to visit once she was well enough.

One of the first weekend outings she made with Bill during her recovery was to Luss.  Seeing the village for real was like stepping into a scene from make-believe.  The quaint cottages, the tiny jetty on the serene loch, and the gentle landscape were very real and captivated her heart.  Mam made several more journeys to Luss and never wavered from the sheer delight she experienced from her visits.  Over and over again, she referred to it as her favourite place and asked me to make sure some of her ashes were scattered from the small jetty on the loch.  Her request was poignant and filled with the deep connection she felt for that beautiful place.

The next five years were a time of joy and precious moments for Mam and our family.  Mam's health remained stable, thanks to effective medication and regular check-ups, allowing her to embrace life fully once again.  With Bill doting on her and showering her with love and care, Mam flourished.

Their three-month holiday to Malta was a dream come true, providing much-needed warmth and relaxation during the winter months.  It was actually cheaper for them both to stay in Malta than to stay in England.  They explored every corner of the island, immersing themselves in new experiences and creating happy memories together.

Mam always made time for me.  With my work schedule of seven nights on and seven off, the weeks I wasn't working became opportunities for us to enjoy each other's company, whether it was exploring new places or simply spending quality time at home.

Family gatherings became more frequent, especially with the arrival of Paul's first child, Maria, in 1992. Three years later, Kate joined the family, bringing even more joy and laughter into our lives.  Mam adored her great-granddaughters, delighting in spoiling them whenever they visited.

One memorable day at Legoland stands out in my mind as special.  Mam and I had a wonderful time with Maria and Kate, walking the park.  The girls made sure they captured every Lego model that was on offer for their eyes to see.  We enjoyed a picnic lunch.  The girls were often uncontrollable at the sights that must have seemed endless to them.  However, it was during this outing that I noticed Mam growing increasingly tired, needing more frequent rests than usual.

In July 1997, following a routine blood test, Mam received a summons from her doctor.  Bill and I accompanied her to the surgery, our minds working overtime with worry, yet clinging to the hope that it was nothing serious.  Little did we know but our lives were again about to be shattered.

The doctor's grave expression told us that something was terribly wrong. He explained that Mam's blood levels were cause for concern and recommended further investigation with a scan. We made our way to the hospital the following week with apprehension, hoping for the best but fearing the worst.

The news we received at the hospital was devastating beyond words. Mam was diagnosed with stage 4 ovarian cancer, and to our horror, the doctors informed us that there were no further treatment options available. The disease had progressed too far and Mam was given a grim prognosis: six months to live.

In that moment, disbelief and anger consumed us. How could this be happening? Mam, a pillar of strength and resilience, now faced an unimaginable battle with an enemy that seemed unbeatable.

Mam´s diagnosis cast a shadow over all our lives and plunged us into a state of profound grief. The natural human thoughts of endless life that we ordinarily feel were changed for ever, and we were left struggling with the harsh reality of mortality.

# Thirty-eight

*W*hen the doctor spoke those fateful words,

"You have six months to live," our world had shattered into a million pieces.  The news was a devastating blow, and every second suddenly became precious.  Minor occasions took on a greater importance, and typical celebrations turned into extravagant affairs.  Birthdays were no longer simple; each event was an opportunity to create lasting memories of happy times.

Mam remained remarkably calm and composed throughout.  Her strength was a support to us all.  She took everything in her stride, always in control, ensuring that she faced whatever was coming with composure and strength.

Her first significant decision was to refuse chemotherapy.  She wanted quality time, not prolonged suffering.  Mam chose to spend her days surrounded by the people she loved.  She managed her time well and enjoyed taking part in family occasions, instead of wasting time fighting a losing battle with invasive treatments.

After the shock of the initial prognosis, something remarkable happened.  Ever the most resilient figure in our lives, Mam decided to treat each day as she always had.  She returned to her routines as best she could with Bill by her side, determined to continue to find comfort in the normality of daily life.  It was as if she refused to let the shadow of her illness darken her days.

Although Mam was approaching her fifth month after her diagnosis, and Christmas was just around the corner, her overall condition was stable.  When I talked to her about Christmas, she mentioned that it would be nice to use this festive time to see friends and acquaintances.  She was fully aware that it might be her last Christmas, but she was adamant to reassure us,

"I'm going nowhere yet, I'm not ready!"

The house smelled of pine and cinnamon, and the twinkling lights on the Christmas tree added a magical glow to the evenings that were soon filled with the sounds of laughter and clinking glasses.  Each visitor brought a unique energy, rekindling old stories and creating new ones.  Mam's eyes sparkled and her face lit up with each new visitor.  It was obvious that she needed this time just to enjoy being alive.

Although she had little money of her own to worry about, she did have her treasured possessions.  Among these, her Royal Doulton ladies were her pride and joy. Just as she had lovingly begun my Brambly Hedge collection, she had also begun creating her own collection of these delicate ladies.

We never had to puzzle about what to get Mam as a present.  Every birthday, Christmas and special occasion became an opportunity to add to her collection.  I remember the gleam in her eyes each time she unwrapped a new lady.  She would carefully remove the tissue paper, her fingers trembling with excitement, and reveal the latest addition to her growing family.  Mam proudly displayed her ladies for everyone to see in her pine cabinet, standing against the wall opposite to her.

But one afternoon, that all changed.

As we enjoyed a slice of lemon drizzle cake, Mam suddenly put her cup of tea down and looked at me with a seriousness that caught me off-guard.

"I have something important to ask," she said, her voice gentle but firm.  "I know this is not going to be easy for you, so I hope you understand why I am asking."  She went on to explain, "I want to give my 'ladies' to my family and friends," she said, "so they have something of mine to keep and remember me by."  At first, her words hit me like a ton of bricks.  I struggled with my emotions, torn between my attachment to the figurines and my understanding of Mam's wishes.  She looked at me with her warm eyes, and I knew that this decision was important to her.  No matter how difficult her request was going to be, I made sure we did it together, just the way Mam wanted.  It was so hard to see the cabinet emptying.  I watched Mam wrap each lady in soft tissue paper and label the gift, making sure it went to the right person on her death. One by one, the ladies found new homes and Mam was content.

What started as a painful process turned into a beautiful, shared experience. Mam's Royal Doulton ladies, once just delicate porcelain figures, transformed into cherished keepsakes.

Mam knew that she might not be around for my next birthday. With this in mind, she secretly liaised with Bill to buy a special Royal Doulton lady as a birthday present, determined to give me one last gift, regardless of the circumstances.

On the morning of my birthday, Bill handed me a beautifully wrapped package.

"This is from Mam," he said softly, his eyes filled with the same mix of sorrow and tenderness that I felt. My hands unsteady, I unwrapped that paper, revealing a delicate box. Inside was a special edition Doulton lady, called 'How Shall I Compare Thee?'.

My emotions were over-whelming. I traced the elegant lines of the figurine, feeling Mam's presence in every detail. Her dress was a shimmering yellow, reminiscent of the summer days we had spent together in the garden. She held a single rose, her face serene and full of grace. Tears streamed down my face as I clutched the figurine to my chest. Despite the sadness of her passing 12 weeks earlier, this moment was proof of her enduring spirit and an example of how she had always found a way to show her love.

Mam had thought of everything, ensuring that, even in her absence, she could still be part of my special day.

Mam and I would sit together in the quieter moments, just the two of us, talking about everything and nothing.  She spoke about her life, her dreams, and her wishes for us after she was gone.  The one thing she feared was my future without her.  She knew she was my rock just as I was hers, but she wanted reassurance that I wouldn't crumble without her.

She often voiced her concern, her eyes searching mine for some reassurance.

"Promise me you'll be strong," she would say, her voice soft but firm.  I always promised, wanting to ease her mind, but the truth was, I was uncertain myself.

What Mam didn't fully realise was that her grit had become part of me over the years.  Her strength and her ability to face adversity had become an inner part of who I was.  Every challenge she met head-on, every moment of calm in the storm, had taught me to be just as resilient.

Thankfully, Mam managed to get through the winter months without too many problems and was now looking forward to springtime.  One beautiful day in early May, Mam and I decided to take a drive to Bradgate Park.  The weather was perfect, with a gentle breeze carrying the fresh scent of blooming flowers and the sun casting a warm glow over the landscape.

Mam's face lit up when we arrived.  She had always loved the spacious tranquillity of the park, and today it seemed even more inviting.  We parked the car and made Mam comfortable in her wheelchair before slowly making our way along one of the winding paths.  Mam was quite happy to sit in her chair and watch the stream flow gently by and see the deer grazing, undisturbed by our presence.

I found a bench by the stream.  As soon as I saw it, I knew it was 'our' bench.  It felt like we had sat there on countless previous visits and, as we settled in, the world around us seemed to pause.

We reminisced about past visits to Bradgate Park, laughing and smiling at the memories.  We recalled the time we came with Auntie Glenis and Uncle John when I was just a young child.  I could vividly remember how Uncle John had helped me climb up to the Old John Tower, the highest point in the park.  To my young mind, I was scaling Everest, and the sense of achievement when we finally reached the top was overwhelming.

Those memories were precious, but they also reminded us of more recent times. We talked about Paul, Gemma and Dave and how they had done exactly the same thing, their faces beaming with pride and excitement as they made the climb.  It was as if history was repeating itself and now here we were, Mam and I, watching other children experiencing the same excitement and adventure.  Our conversation flowed as easily as the stream beside us, touching on everything from family stories to hopes and dreams for the future.

But the biggest giggle we shared that day was when we remembered my broken big toe incident.  It had been a very warm August Bank Holiday when Tony, our three children, Mam and I all decided to pay a visit to Bradgate Park.  Although the park was teeming with people, its vast expanse made it feel almost empty.

I was walking on the grass, watching the kids head for the stream, when my foot got caught in a rabbit hole. As I pulled my foot free, I knew instantly that my big toe was broken.  I hopped over to the stream and plunged my foot into the cold water to ease the pain and swelling.

The sight of my impromptu hopping drew a crowd, and one of the cyclists nearby decided to alert the park ranger.  Within ten minutes, I found myself being hauled into the back of the park ranger's Land Rover truck, with my family in tow (excuse the pun).

It got worse!  As we reached the gates to the car park, I could hear the sound of sirens.  To my astonishment, an ambulance with its blue lights flashing was coming for me.  You can imagine how embarrassing it was with what seemed like hundreds of people gathered to watch the spectacle unfold.  At the time, it was mortifying, but as the years went by, the more we told the story, the funnier it became.

Today was no exception.  As Mam and I recalled the event, we were in stitches, laughing so hard that tears streamed down our faces.  The image of me being carted off, surrounded by a bemused crowd, had turned from a moment of pain and embarrassment into one of our fondest, funniest memories.

Mam asked if we could go and see the ruins, as she was always interested in the park's history.  We moved further along the path and reached the picturesque ruins of Bradgate House where Lady Jane Grey was born in 1537.  Legend has it that, following her execution, Jane walked along the house walls at night with her head under her arm.  This was a place where, as a child, I would also walk along the low walls of the ruins and create my own imaginary adventures, but with my head firmly fixed to my shoulders.

After a while, Mam began to feel tired, so we decided it was time to head home.  We slowly walked back to the car park, enjoying the lingering peace.

Just as we were about to leave, we spotted the 'Oki Man' (good old Leicester slang for an ice cream man) in his van, both of us saying simultaneously,

"Shall we have an oki with nuts and raz (raspberry sauce)?" It was as though we were reading each other's thoughts. We laughed, delighted by the simple pleasure that had become a family tradition. We sat in the car enjoying each lick. The cool sweetness was refreshing, a perfect end to our visit. When we had finished our ice creams, I started the drive home. Glancing over at Mam, I saw that her eyes were closed and she had a beautiful contented smile on her face.

Having the willpower to survive for sixteen months was amazing, but it was now evident that Mam was struggling with her breathing and her pain was worsening. The signs of her deteriorating condition were becoming impossible to ignore. Her doctor ordered that piped oxygen be installed in Mam and Bill's flat, ensuring that her wish to remain in her home could be fulfilled.

On good days, with her oxygen flowing from a portable tank, we would return to our roots in Leicester and visit our favourite café, Brucciani's. We enjoyed a cup of coffee and relished one of their famous cream buns. Each visit to the café was like a small victory, a credit to Mam's spirit and determination. The familiar surroundings of Brucciani's, with its cosy atmosphere, had brought immense pleasure to our lives over the years, and was still doing so.  The staff, recognising us as regulars, always greeted Mam with warm smiles and extra care which made these outings even more special.

In her final months, Mam taught us an invaluable lesson about living.  She showed us that bravery isn't always about fighting; sometimes, it's about choosing how you live your life.  Mam became our support, guiding us through the depths of our emotions without us even realising it.  She chose to face her mortality with dignity and, in doing so, she gave us the greatest gift of all: the understanding that every moment is precious and that the beauty of life lies in the ordinary days we often take for granted.

As Mam's strength weakened and her grip on life loosened, she looked at me with eyes filled with love and whispered those words I had both dreaded and anticipated:

"It's time."

My heart clenched with sorrow but, above all, I wanted Mam to find peace, to be free from the pain that had haunted her in her final days.  With trembling hands, I reached for the phone to call the doctor, knowing deep down that this would mark the end of our time together.

But before I could dial the number, Mam squeezed my hand and made a request that took me by surprise.

She wanted me to ask Paul, her eldest grandson, to bring her two little great-grandchildren, Maria and Kate, to her side.

I made the call, tears threatening to spill down my cheeks as I summoned the strength to carry out Mam's final wish. Moments later, Paul arrived with Maria, aged 7, and Kate, aged 4, their innocent faces a stark contrast to the sombreness of the occasion. Their liveliness filled the space with a marked energy, momentarily easing the grief that hung heavy in the air. Kate's eyes widened with fascination as she spotted Mam's adjustable chair, eager to explore its mechanical wonders. It was Maria who approached Mam first, her small hand grasping Mam's with a tenderness far beyond her years. In that moment, time paused as four generations intertwined in a beautiful embrace.

And then, as if on cue, Maria and Kate's infectious laughter filled the room, their innocent joy a glow of light in the darkness. They had one simple request: a tea party with their 'Nana Els'. With tears streaming down my face, I watched as Mam's face lit up with a beautiful smile, her pain momentarily forgotten as she shared the laughter and love. And as Maria poured imaginary tea into mismatched cups and Kate nibbled on imaginary biscuits, I realised that in that moment, Mam had found her peace.

For in the midst of sorrow, there was beauty.  In the midst of pain, there was love.  And in the midst of goodbye, there was a tea party, a fleeting moment of joy that would forever be etched in my heart as a reminder of the extraordinary power of love to exceed even the darkest of moments.

Mam had defied the odds for 21 months.  She displayed her greatest courage while she prepared for her own death.

What a remarkable lady she was.

# Thirty-nine

*A*t 6.30 pm on the evening of Monday, 19th April 1999, the light of my world was extinguished.

Mam took her final breath and found peace.

She left behind a legacy of intrepid strength and unconditional love.